Self-Determination

A Tribute to Rich Simpson

Dr. Richard L. Simpson unexpectedly passed away just as this series was about to go to press. He had a significant and profound impact on each of us, the field of special education, and the areas of autism and behavior disorders in particular. Dr. Simpson spent 42 years of his career at the University of Kansas, from where he led the field in developing teacher preparation programs for future educators of students with autism and behavior disorders. He also conducted research to identify scientifically validated practices, and published over 200 articles, books, and book chapters. His work guided the field's effort to bridge the gap between research and practice and advanced the movement to identify and use evidence-based practices that improved the lives of children and youth with autism and their families. Many revered Dr. Simpson. His numerous awards and public recognitions reflect a distinguished career of considerable contribution.

Dr. Simpson was also a remarkable and inspiring teacher and mentor. His knowledge was awe-inspiring, yet he was approachable and personable. He supported graduate students by providing them with many opportunities to publish and conduct research and to complete professional presentations and school-based consultations. His students will carry his legacy throughout the world, working as teachers, school administrators, consultants, researchers, and professors, all serving children and youth with autism and their families.

Those who knew Dr. Simpson will remember his friendly and caring disposition, great sense of humor, and quick wit. He was a wonderful friend to many, and his guidance and encouragement were unparalleled. He will be missed by many, in ways that are too numerous to count.

PRO-ED Series on Autism Spectrum Disorders
Second Edition

Edited by Richard L. Simpson

Titles in the Series

Visual Supports–Second Edition

Discrete Trial Training–Second Edition

Naturalistic and Incidental Teaching–Second Edition

Verbal Behavior–Second Edition

Social Skills and Social Interactions–Second Edition

Assistive and Instructional Technology

Sexuality Education

Self-Management and Cognitive Behavioral Interventions

Functional Behavioral Assessment

Self-Determination

PRO-ED Series on Autism Spectrum Disorders
Second Edition

Self-Determination

Karrie A. Shogren

Michael L. Wehmeyer

8700 Shoal Creek Boulevard
Austin, Texas 78757-6897
800/897-3202 Fax 800/397-7633
www.proedinc.com

8700 Shoal Creek Boulevard
Austin, Texas 78757-6897
800/897-3202 Fax 800/397-7633
www.proedinc.com

Library of Congress Cataloging-in-Publication Data
Control Number: 2017053097 (print)

Art Director: Jason Crosier
Designer: Lissa Hattersley
This book is designed in Nexus Serif TF and Formata Sans.

Printed in the United States of America

1 2 3 4 5 6 7 8 9 10 27 26 25 24 23 22 21 20 19 18

Contents

From the Editor

Children and youth with autism spectrum disorder (ASD) routinely demonstrate exceptionally demanding and distinctive characteristics and needs. Even when compared to other disabilities, ASD is especially complex and perplexing. Learners diagnosed with ASD exhibit a range of cognitive, communicative, and social–emotional interests and abilities; and they commonly display a variety of challenging behaviors. Still, many children and adolescents with ASD have normal patterns of growth and development, a wide range of distinctive assets and capabilities, and some individuals with ASD have highly developed and inimitable abilities. These widely varied and unique features necessitate specially designed interventions and strategies orchestrated by knowledgeable and skilled professionals. When supported by the right combination of well-informed professionals (and in many instances parents and family members) and appropriate methods and intervention strategies, children and youth with ASD show significant progress. Without a doubt, consistent and correct use of effective methods, as presented in the current series, is the key to achieving successful outcomes with individuals with ASD.

Preface to the Series

Identification, correct implementation, and ongoing evaluation of scientifically supported and effective practices are essential features of effective programming for learners with ASD. Unquestionably, there is a clear-cut link between use of interventions and supports with empirical backing and positive school and post-school outcomes. Different terms, including *evidence-based procedures and practices, scientifically supported interventions*, and *research-validated methods*, all refer to methods and practices that have been successful in bringing about desired changes based on objective and empirically valid research Unfortunately, practitioners all too often fail to use these proven tools and procedures, or use them the wrong way.

Indeed, this "research-to-practice gap" is a major obstacle in efficiently and effectively addressing the needs of learners with ASD and creating optimal pathways to the best outcomes. This is not a problem of motivation, intent, or objective. Educators and other professionals, as well as parents, families, and other stakeholders, want the most effective methods and updated ASD information. Regrettably, clearly written and practitioner- and family-friendly materials that provide straightforward and user-friendly information and explanations are in short supply.

This concern was the motivation for creating the current resources. Each book in the series provides utilitarian and down-to-earth information on using an intervention or support method with potential to produce significant benefit. Each book, written in a user-friendly and straightforward fashion by experienced internationally recognized professionals, offers practical information, solutions, and strategies for successfully supporting individuals with ASD and related disabilities.

The 10 books in the series offer clear and direct guidance on applying research-supported and proven information, methods, and procedures. The series has the potential to make a significant positive difference for teachers and allied professionals.

Several of the books focus on using applied behavior analysis (ABA), the single most verified intervention tool for learners with ASD. The revised series includes the following:

- De Boer provides step-by-step use of discrete trial instruction and related methodology.
- Sturmey provides guidance on implementing ABA-based verbal behavior methodology.
- Tincani, Lorah, and Dowdy direct readers in how to design maximally effective management programs via functional behavior assessment and analysis.

Other skill development foci are covered in the series, each with an emphasis on practical application of documented methods, as evidenced in the following:

- Stichter and Conroy address the ever-pressing issue of building social skill assets among children and youth with ASD and harnessing the support of peers.
- Charlop provides a practitioner-friendly explanation of use of naturalistic teaching strategies and incidental teaching methods.
- Ayres and Whiteside provide essential and utilitarian information on how to take advantage of assistive and instructional-technology tools to teach and support learners with ASD.
- Earles-Vollrath, Cook, and Kemper, in detail, describe efficacious visual supports that can help children and youth with ASD function more effectively and independently.

- Crutchfield and Wood provide readers clear-cut instruction in the use of cognitive behavior modification, self-management, and self-monitoring methods.
- Shogren and Wehmeyer, via their book on self-determination, offer specific and clearly described strategies for ensuring individuals with ASD are fully and deservedly involved in their program plans and outcomes.
- Finally, Travers addresses the all-too-often-neglected topic of sexuality matters among adolescents and young adults with autism-related disabilities.

Richard L. Simpson
Series Editor

1 Introduction

Promoting self-determination has been shown to improve school and transition outcomes for students with disabilities, including students with autism spectrum disorder (ASD). The methods, materials, and strategies described in this book will benefit teachers and other direct-support personnel, as well as other members of support teams (including family members and friends), and enable them to support children and youth with ASD in acquiring the skills that enable them to become more self-determined. Research has validated multiple methods, materials, and strategies to promote the skills, knowledge, and beliefs leading to enhanced self-determination (Algozzine, Browder, Karvonen, Test, & Wood, 2001; Wehmeyer, Palmer, Shogren, Williams-Diehm, & Soukup, 2013; Wehmeyer et al., 2012). These methods, materials, and strategies will be the focus of the following chapters and can be individualized to learners with ASD with a wide range of support needs throughout childhood and adolescence.

The importance of promoting the self-determination of students with ASD and related developmental disabilities has been well established in the research literature. Research has found that promoting self-determination results in more positive outcomes with respect to school, post-school employment, postsecondary education, and community living (Shogren, Lee, & Panko, 2016; Shogren, Wehmeyer, Palmer, Rifenbark, & Little, 2015; Test et al., 2009). The importance of self-determination for students with ASD (Wehmeyer, Shogren, Zager, Smith, & Simpson, 2010) has been specifically noted, and, given recent research (Chou, Wehmeyer, Palmer, & Lee, in press) suggesting that students with ASD report lower levels of self-determination than same-age peers with intellectual disability or learning disabilities, the need for instruction to promote self-determination for students with ASD becomes all the more pressing. Understanding the unique support needs of each student and adopting a life span focus are key to efforts to enhance skills, knowledge, and beliefs leading to greater self-determination. This focus introduces opportunities throughout pre-K, primary, and secondary education years to enable and support students with ASD to build the knowledge, skills, and beliefs leading to the development of self-determination (Wehmeyer & Shogren, in press-a).

The unique instructional and support needs of children and youth with ASD related to communication and social interactions must be considered in designing and implementing interventions to promote self-determination, as this book describes. Considering appropriate supports for communication and social interactions when teaching complex skills like social problem solving or self-advocacy will be important. However, promoting self-determination can provide natural opportunities for students to learn more about their communication and social support needs and to advocate and set goals for enhancing their skills in these areas. It should be noted, however, that the focus should be not just on teaching students knowledge and skills leading to enhanced self-determination but also on changing the environments in which children and youth with ASD live and learn. Doing so will help them create meaningful opportunities for practicing these skills and developing perceptions and beliefs about themselves and their capacities that lead them to act in self-determined ways. Research has consistently found that when supports and opportunities are provided to enhance self-determination, all students, including students with ASD, can acquire knowledge and skills that lead to enhanced self-determination. Strategies for providing supports for the use of these skills are highlighted in each of the following chapters. It is also important to note that teaching skills or creating opportunities in only one context is not enough to enable the development of self-determination; instead, it is critical to provide opportunities and supports across environments. Further, collaborative relationships between families, teachers, and students are necessary to ensure communication and alignment of efforts to promote skills leading to self-determination and opportunities to practice those skills across home and school environments.

When thinking about supports that promote self-determination, what is known about effective supports (e.g., visual supports, technology-based solutions, antecedent cues) for students with ASD, in general, can provide important strategies for individualizing instruction to promote self-determination. Applying this knowledge allows practitioners to individualize instruction and use their knowledge of effective supports for the students they work with to create and enhance opportunities for self-determination.

Defining Self-Determination

Self-determination is defined as acting as the causal agent in one's life (Shogren, Wehmeyer, Palmer, Forber-Pratt, et al., 2015). *Causal agents* are people who make or cause things to happen in their lives; they engage in actions that move them toward their goals. These actions are volitional (i.e., based on choices and preferences and self-directed) and agentic (i.e., reflect an understanding of pathways that can be used to make change and are self-regulated). Causal agents also see a link between their actions and the outcomes they experience, leading to them feel empowered and able to use self-awareness and self-knowledge to make progress toward goals.

There are a number of specific skills, beliefs, and attitudes that enable people to act as causal agents in their lives and that promote the development of self-determination. It is the acquisition and development of these skills, beliefs, and attitudes across the life span that lead to the ability to engage in self-determined actions. These skills, beliefs, and attitudes include choice-making skills, decision-making and problem-solving skills, self-advocacy skills, goal-setting and attainment skills, self-regulation skills, and self-awareness and self-knowledge. We focus on strategies to teach and create opportunities for each of these skills, beliefs, and abilities in the following chapters. We also introduce a model of instruction, the *Self-Determined Learning Model of Instruction* (SDLMI), which can be used by teachers and other support persons to teach multiple skills leading to greater self-determination. The skills and attitudes discussed in the following chapters can be taught simultaneously, although they also build on each other, so depending on a student's current skills and abilities, instruction on specific skills may be introduced sequentially (e.g., beginning with instruction on choice-making skills, then providing instruction on problem-solving and, then, decision-making skills) or may be taught simultaneously or in combination with a multicomponent intervention like the SDLMI.

Because assessment is inextricably linked to instruction, there are several assessments that measure self-determination. For example, *The Arc's Self-Determination Scale* (SDS; Wehmeyer & Kelchner, 1995) and the *AIR Self-Determination Scale* (AIR; Wolman, Campeau, Dubois, Mithaug, & Stolarski, 1994) are both global measures of self-determination. The SDS has 72 items and is a student self-report measure. Scores for autonomy, self-regulation, psychological empowerment, and self-realization, as well as for overall self-determination, can be calculated. The *AIR Self-Determination Scale* assesses student capacity and opportunity for self-determination. The AIR has student, educator, and parent versions so that multiple perspectives on a student's self-determination can be obtained. The AIR Capacity subscale asks about things that students do and feel related to self-determined behavior, and the Opportunity subscale assesses opportunities for self-determined behavior at home and school. Shogren and colleagues (2017) have developed a new suite of tools to assess self-determination through online administration called the *Self-Determination Inventory System,* which includes a student report (*Self-Determination Inventory: Student-Report* or SDI: SR) and an adult report (*Self-Determination Inventory: Parent/Teacher Report* or PTR) version. These two versions include some items from the SDS, as well as new items reflecting emerging knowledge and research related to assessment of self-determination. The measure is available at http://www.self-determination.org. The online version incorporates multiple universal design features to promote accessibility to a wide range of students (e.g., slider rating scale, word definitions, questions, read-aloud functions), including students with ASD (who were included in the norming sample). Determining the appropriate assessment will depend on the needs of the student (e.g., is online assessment appropriate) and the goal of assessment (e.g., is the teacher interested in gathering multiple perspectives, is there an interest in understanding capacity and opportunity or self-determination characteristics). Gathering data on a student's self-determination can be a useful way to identify skills to target for instruction. Repeating assessments of self-determination across time can also provide ongoing data about changes based on instruction.

2 Choice-Making Skills

If being self-determined means acting volitionally (and it does!), then among the first areas of intervention would be to promote and support choice making. Expressing preferences and making choices are important across the life span, but, with regard to the development of self-determination, are particularly important in early childhood and early elementary. The types of choice opportunities can be individualized to different situations, and increasingly consequential choices can be introduced as children age after a strong foundation for communicating preferences is laid early in life. Researchers have found that creating opportunities for basic choices early in life (e.g., the order of activities, timing of activities) can impact engagement and reduce problem behavior, creating a foundation for the development of other skills leading to self-determination as well as greater engagement in academic learning. The power of allowing and promoting choice-making opportunities in education is probably underrecognized. In a compelling illustration of this, Dominguez et al. (2013) studied the relationship between choice opportunities, preference, and the actual vegetable consumption of 4- to 6-year-old children. In one experimental condition, children chose a vegetable to eat before their meal. In the second condition, children were provided multiple vegetables during the meal and could choose a vegetable at any time. There was also a no-choice condition, where children were given only one vegetable. Both choice conditions resulted in significantly higher vegetable intake than the no-choice condition, even when the no-choice condition included a vegetable that the child had identified as their favorite vegetable. For young children, providing choices motivates them to engage and act. For older students, making choices becomes an expectation of adolescence and a marker of maturity.

Teaching Choice-Making Skills

There are two distinct components of the choice-making process that are important to think about when teaching and creating opportunities for choice making. Making choices involves identifying a preference and communicating that preference (Reid, Parsons, & Green, 1991). Students with ASD may need support in one or both of these areas. To identify preferences, students must have experiences that enable them to understand what they prefer. They must also have a reliable means of communicating their preferences. This can be verbal, gestural, or through a communication system. If they have no other way to communicate their thoughts and preferences, some children may act in ways that could be construed as problem behaviors to communicate their preferences. This is why creating a consistent means for children to express preference and communicate choices can be very important for children with ASD.

When thinking about supporting students with ASD to identify their preferences, it is important to remember that a key part of developing preferences is having experiences with the items/activities/events. Think about how you have developed preferences for foods, for types of recreation activities, for work, and so forth. For example, you probably tasted different types of foods at various points in your life and began to identify those that you liked more and less than others. And, your food preferences have probably changed over time. The same can be said for different leisure, recreation, or exercise activities, or, even, with your preferences for your career and your social relationships.

As a person supporting children and youth with ASD, a first step to creating opportunities for choice making is designing opportunities for exposure to a diverse array of experiences and activities. There are many ways to achieve this. You can use structured preference assessments to learn more about what children and youth prefer and use this information to create instructional opportunities. Preference assessments can be used to learn more about what a student prefers to eat or to do for fun, as well as for what types of instructional activities and materials are most engaging, which can be an indication of preference. You can then use this knowledge to create choice-making opportunities to promote engagement in classroom and instructional activities. For example, if you identify a variety of activities that a student participates in, you can then create opportunities for the student to choose the order of activities, the peers he or she works with on activities, or the materials the student uses to complete activities. You can add in new options each day so that the student is exposed to more activities and increases his or her experiences and range of responses. Only through exposure to multiple experiences can students begin to reliably identify their preferences and interests.

Across the life span, but particularly as students with ASD enter early adolescence, it is important to create opportunities to make choices and assess preferences linked to career-related activities and other post-school education and community living outcomes. For example, creating opportunities to visit and experience different types of vocational settings and activities and different college environments can help students identify preferences and begin to express preferences about their future. Because many students with ASD benefit from concrete experiences and examples, it can be particularly useful to ensure that students are exposed to representations of these different activities (e.g., videos, pictures) and well as real-world opportunities to visit settings and participate in events as students may respond differently to actual activities in the environment that are not fully captured in representations, such as pictures and videos. It is also critically important to get the student's perspective when assessing preferences. While getting input from family members and others who know the person well can help narrow down the activities that will be assessed, researchers have found that there are often differences in the preferences related to work activities, for example, expressed by young people with disabilities and those that support them (Agran & Krupp, 2011). However, it is also important to be creative when identifying opportunities for students with ASD to sample and experience, because if a student does not have experience with a potential career or living option, he or she will be unable to express a meaningful preference.

Assessing Preferences

Formal procedures exist for assessing preferences, particularly for students with extensive support needs. Preference assessments can be direct or indirect. Indirect assessments typically involve asking someone else about a student's preferences. As mentioned previously, this can be a good starting point for identifying things to include in a direct preference assessment. But, direct assessment is also important because other people may not always be aware of a person's preferences. And, if the young person has not yet experienced different options, it may be difficult—even for a person who knows the young person well—to identify preferences.

Methods of conducting a direct assessment are usually characterized as approach-based or engagement-based (Hagopian, Long, & Rush, 2004). In *approach-based assessments*, you might put a single item (i.e., single-item presentation), two items (i.e., paired-item presentation), or multiple items (i.e., multiple-item presentation or mass-trial presentation) in front of the student and see which item the student interacts with. This type of preference assessment can be helpful to determine preferences for foods, materials, and other items that are easily manipulated. This can also be a good opportunity to create ways for students to interact with different materials and objects. For example, prior to an approach-based assessment, providing students with free access to the materials that will be used can be important to enable a meaningful assessment if students are not familiar with all of the materials. During an assessment, you should record whether the student *approaches* the item (e.g., reaches for it, says they want it, activates a microswitch) and keep track of the number of times this occurs.

Engagement-based assessments work well for more activity-based experiences, where involvement over a longer period of time is used to document preferences.

For example, engagement-based approaches can be can be used to assess vocational preferences, social activity preferences, recreation and leisure activities, and other events. You record how long the student engages with the activity or with the materials and look for differences across activities to explore which items are preferred.

When supporting students to develop and express preferences using approach or engagement, a critical element is to create multiple opportunities for interactions with activities and items. As students have repeated exposure, they become better able to express preferences and make choices. And, in making choices and expressing preferences, they become aware that multiple modalities may be used to express preferences. Choices and preference can be expressed verbally, through gestures, through pencil and paper, through technology, and even behaviorally. More than likely, some combination of these approaches may be used. For example, a student might state that he is interested in one type of career, but after taking a vocational assessment or visiting a job site, he may show through his engagement that he is more interested in other activities. Being aware and sensitive to these various responses enables children and youth with ASD to see that people in the world see and recognize their preferences, and enable them to feel more empowered to express those preferences. Considering the unique support needs of individual students with ASD—particularly related to their need for concrete representations, for exposure to activities to understand the demands of these activities, and the role of communication and social interactions in expressing preferences—is crucial for success.

Various tools exist, particularly related to vocational-preferences assessment, which can be useful. For example, there are paper-and-pencil assessments that support young people to identify and rank possible career options. Technology-based programs have also been created that enable students to watch videos or look at pictures of various job activities and identify those that they prefer. Remember, however, that the abstractness of paper-and-pencil or picture or video assessments can be a challenge for some students, and all students—particularly for high-stakes decisions, like what career path they want to pursue—should be supported to have real hands-on experiences with potential options, as these experiences enhance one's understanding of preferences.

To enable students to express their choices, or to take action on their preferences, it is important to ensure that they learn to express—in their preferred modality—their preferences, as well as appropriate ways to take action on those preferences. For students who communicate verbally, this might involve instruction in when and how to communicate preferences in social situations. For students who use high- or low-tech communication systems, it is important to ensure access to pictures or other tools to express preferences. For example, a student who uses a picture-based communication system will not be able to use this system to communicate a choice if appropriate pictures are not available. Technology tools, where multiple pictures can be loaded and students and/or their support persons can sort through them and pull up certain pictures to create choice opportunities, are emerging that can create meaningful access and opportunities for expression. Remember, too, that it might take time for students to learn to use such pictures or situations to express preferences and make choices. For example, one student, who was working with a technology-based system where his support team was putting pictures on the screen for him to express what he wanted to do next, was picking one picture that they strongly believed to represent a nonpreferred activity. However, he consistently touched or pointed to the less preferred choice. His family thought that he was just interested in the picture and took him to experience the activity. After an opportunity to engage in the activity, he stopped picking this picture and began selecting the preferred activity consistently. In this case, it took multiple experiences and instructional trials for the student to see the connection between the pictures, his pointing at it, and the outcome he experienced. But, once he made this connection, he was able to generalize it to expressing his preferences by selecting pictures across multiple activities and choices. His family and teachers also focused on ensuring he had experiences with activities that were added to the pictures available on his communication system.

This brings up something important to keep in mind: Preferences are likely to change over time, particularly as children and youth have new and different experiences or as popular activities, styles, or options change. For these reasons, it is important to frequently reassess preferences and to always focus on creating new experiences that enable preferences to be developed and choices to be expressed. Preferences for things like instructional materials, for example, can change very frequently and should be assessed routinely as a part of instruction. For longer term activities and experiences, ongoing experience and exposure to various career options, community living options, and social activities will be important. Also, the types of supports for social activities and communication that children prefer should be routinely examined as children grow, develop, and have new experiences. The ultimate goal of supporting choice making and preference expression is to enable students to use this knowledge to act on their environments and to support this through instruction and supports planning. In doing so, students become empowered to express themselves, taking action through choice making, and seeing the connection between their actions and the outcomes they experience. Starting this process early in life creates early opportunities for the development of the skills associated with the development of self-determination.

Creating Choice-Making Opportunities

Shevin and Klein (1984), in an early article on choice making, suggested the importance of the following steps to enhance choice opportunities over time:

1. Incorporate student choice early in instruction;
2. Increase the number of decisions the student makes;
3. Increase the number of domains (e.g., areas, fields) in which decisions are made;
4. Raise the significance in terms of risk and long-term consequences; and
5. Clearly communicate with the student concerning areas of possible choice and the limits within which choices can be made.

This list highlights the importance of thinking about choice and preference throughout the life span and systematically planning to increase choice opportunities and the consequences of choice over time.

"Low risk" choices are important over the life span and can include choices about things ranging from what pencil or color pen to use to what extracurricular activities to pursue. With age, choices can get more complicated, but such complexity provides natural opportunities for students to learn more about the consequences and outcomes of their choices. Participating in educational planning as a member of the Individualized Education Program (IEP) team as well as in transition planning and other instructional and postsecondary decisions creates a context for students to be part of a team making "higher risk choices" in a supportive context, as they begin to learn to use skills like decision making and problem solving that are described in the next chapter.

Ultimately, opportunities for developing preferences and expressing choices are available across contexts and activities. However, research has found that opportunities across the life span are more restricted for students with disabilities, including students with ASD. So, when planning instruction and supports, think carefully about how you can embed choice making and preferences expression opportunities across the instructional day. There is an array of options for creating more choice opportunities and for enabling students to examine the pros and cons of different choices. Students can choose:

- Between instructional activities
- The order of activities
- Not to participate in an activity
- Location of an activity
- Materials/reinforcers
- Learning goals and objectives
- Within the context of education/transition planning

Brainstorm how to plan for choice-making opportunities in your interactions with children and youth with ASD. Plan for tracking data on engagement as an indication of preferences and changes in behavior as students become more skilled in expressing preferences and choices. As young children develop additional and more effective choice-making skills, introducing concepts related to decision making and problem solving can be a natural next step in instruction.

3 Problem-Solving and Decision-Making Skills

As students learn about their preferences and begin to express those preferences by making choices, teachers should think about introducing instruction related to promoting problem solving and decision making. When students begin to evaluate the pros and cons of different choices and use this information to guide them in their actions, they are using decision-making skills, and as they encounter problems in identifying possible decision options, implementing decisions, or navigating barriers in the environment, they need to use problem-solving skills. Although the terms *choice, decision*, and *problem* are often used interchangeably, they actually refer to distinct processes that can be directly taught to enhance student self-determination. The previous chapter reviewed strategies to assess preferences and promote choice-making opportunities. This chapter focuses on teaching and creating opportunities for problem-solving and decision-making skills.

Promoting Problem-Solving Skills

Problems are encountered in all domains of life, and developing strategies to identify and navigate problems encountered is a critical skill to enable students to be causal agents and engage in agentic action. A *problem* can be defined as any activity or task for which a solution is not known or readily apparent. Problems can emerge for multiple reasons. Children and youth might encounter problems in reaching a goal they have set, they might encounter problems in making decisions, or they might encounter barriers in their environment that they need to navigate (e.g., they cannot access something they want or need). Children and youth will sometimes be able to readily identify solutions and will, at other times, need more support. But most students need support to learn to evaluate solutions and select the best solution aligned with their goals and interests.

Younger children are not developmentally ready to solve problems, but there are activities that can prepare students in their late-elementary years and during early middle school/junior high for problem solving. Like most other social skills, modeling problem-solving strategies, both at school and home, and involving young children in discussions about problems can prepare them for later problem-solving skill acquisition. The intent of such role modeling and discussions involves showing children that problems can be addressed and engaging them in means–end analyses (that is, the consideration of how various means to a problem solution can resolve problem situations). It is in the later elementary and early secondary years that students develop the ability to cognitively understand and process problem situations. Thus, explicit instruction on problem-solving skills begins during this time frame.

To solve a problem, the following steps are generally identified as important when attempting to identify, generate, and evaluate potential problem solutions:

1. Identify and define the problem.
2. List possible solutions.
3. Identify the impact of each solution.
4. Make a judgment about a preferred solution.
5. Evaluate the efficacy of the judgment.

Teaching each of these steps through modeling, role-play, and explicit instruction will enable students with ASD to develop their problem-solving skills. The first step, identifying and defining the problem, is particularly important, because recognizing when there is a problem is critical to moving forward with solving the problem. Recognizing problems is important to navigate social situations, to communicate effectively, and to use many of the other skills described in this book. Sometimes students may recognize there is a problem, but may struggle with defining the parameters of the problem. Students can learn questions to ask themselves to clarify the problem and develop the skills to clearly state the problem. For example, questions like: (a) Is the problem caused by me or someone else? and (b) How important is the problem? can be useful in enabling students to define the problem. Such questions can also help identify the seriousness of the problem, the information and supports that might need to be accessed, and the amount of time needed to address the problem.

Students' ability to identify solutions will be influenced by experiences and the degree to which possible solutions are known or have been explained. That is why, as a teacher or support person, verbalizing the steps you take in solving a problem or modeling the problem-solving process repeatedly can be important. Using terms like *problem*, *solution*, and *judgment* can help identify the steps being taken and provide examples of how the steps just described are used. Many young people with ASD will require explicit instruction, beyond just listening to the modeling of problem-solving skills, to understand the steps. An explicit focus on generalizing across situations and types of problems will likely also be necessary. In addition to teacher or other support persons modeling the problem-solving process, video modeling and video self-modeling can also be used to provide examples of identifying problems and generating solutions for students with ASD.

After generating solutions, identifying the impact of each solution will require another step that requires that students identify and recognize the potential consequences of the solution. Encouraging students to think through the impact of the solution on them as well as on others (e.g., peers, family, teachers) can be useful at this step. Identifying the preferred solution requires that students experience various solutions and have knowledge of themselves and their preferences. Creating opportunities for students to make choices and experience various consequences, then talking through the potential outcomes of the choices, can help students identify what is preferred for them and evaluate if they have selected the best solution for themselves.

Developing the skills associated with social problem solving for children and youth with ASD may require particular supports, as research suggests that many students may have specific difficulties understanding social and emotional cues and in generating solutions to social problems. However, with instruction in the steps described above, students can learn to generate and evaluate the utility of different solutions. More focus may need to be directed to social situations, especially those that are abstract and require the consideration of contextual cues and events. The importance of such instruction cannot be overstated, however, as increases in social interactions with peers have been observed after social problem-solving instruction (Bauminger, 2007), suggesting the benefits of explicitly teaching social-problems skills for students with ASD.

Benjamin (1996) identified four steps that could be taught to students so that they begin to think about problems encountered at school. These steps include:

1. *Understand*: Students are taught to identify and analyze a situation, to identify the problem, and to name the problem. Teaching techniques can include role-play and modeling.
2. *Plan and solve*: Students learn about how to generate possible options, and how to access resources to identify options they have not thought of.
3. *Check*: The student is taught how to select a solution and check to see whether this has addressed the problem. If not, what else needs to change?
4. *Review*: Students learn how they can generalize these steps to other problems they may encounter in the future.

Considering the complexity of problems is also important both in problem-solving instruction and in supporting students to use problem-solving skills. Problems can be understood as simple or complex. For simple problems, there is a finite solution, and it can be easier to generate and implement solutions for these types of problems. Complex problem solving occurs when situations are dynamic and changeable, requiring novel solutions and the use of various cognitive skills related to gathering information. Complex problems can also be associated with greater uncertainty and risk, necessitating a focus on these concepts. Social problems tend to be complex, but other problems encountered in academic life can also fall into this category. Explicitly teaching the concepts of uncertainty and risk, providing multiple examples of these types of problems, and providing strategies to address problems that include uncertainty and risk is necessary. Processing emotions that may emerge in response to uncertainty and risk and devising strategies to manage and navigate these emotions should be a part of instruction related to complex problems.

Teaching Decision-Making Skills

At its core, decision making involves making choices among competing courses of action (Hickson & Khemka, 2013). Decision making, which includes elements of both choice making and problem solving, developmentally emerges in early adolescence. Key to the process of making decisions is judging which solution is best at a given time, and so requires understanding of the context and environmental demands that necessitate decisions. This involves:

1. Recognizing the circumstances that create a need for a decision,
2. Becoming aware that a decision needs to be made,
3. Identifying the goal or outcome that the decision will influence,
4. Identifying the alternative options,
5. Identifying the consequences of each alternative,
6. Determining the chances of each consequence occurring,
7. Identifying the impact of each action and consequence, and
8. Determining the most attractive action (Wehmeyer & Shogren, in press-b).

To support students with ASD to learn decision-making skills, a number of strategies to teach and create opportunities should be implemented across the life span. One consideration for students with ASD is that decision making can be associated with uncertainty (Beyth-Marom, Fischhoff, Quadrel, & Furby, 1991), and for students with ASD this can become a challenge. Thus, providing discrete instruction on what uncertainty is, how to manage the emotions associated with it, and how to evaluate alternatives when there is uncertainty in outcomes can be useful. Beyth-Marom et al. (1991) suggested discussing different kinds of uncertainty and how to reduce uncertainty by gaining more knowledge. Concepts related to probability and evaluating the chances that something will occur can be introduced at this point. For some students, simple bar and pie graphs can be used to communicate these ideas, building on math skills that students are learning in other contexts. However, decision researchers emphasize that identifying potential consequences is often a "best guess situation" and that students need to learn to evaluate the risk of various decision options. Teaching students how to evaluate and conceptualize risk and comfortable levels of risk in terms of short-term and long-term consequences is important; that taking risks can create opportunities for positive life experiences should be a point of discussion and instruction. Teaching students about low- versus high-risk decisions in a way that links to examples in their lives can help ensure that students understand how to evaluate the impact of different actions. Providing concrete example that relate to each student's life is more helpful than discussing abstract examples.

It is also important to consider family and cultural preferences when teaching decision-making skills. Families vary in the degree to which they emphasize independence and interdependence in decision making, and in future versus present orientations when evaluating risks. Facilitating conversations with family members and learning about how decision making is taught and supported in the home is likewise important. Additionally, when teaching and creating opportunities for decision making, issues related to knowledge and past experience must be considered. Namely, do students have knowledge of the behaviors or consequences they can use in selecting the most relevant action? Also, a key part of decision making is access to knowledgeable sources. This can include people who can provide input and advice on decisions as well as access to information sources (e.g., the internet or books) that provide more information about consequences. Learning to seek help when it is necessary and about appropriate ways to ask for help should be a focus in decision-making instruction.

Finally, decision-making skills can be taught generally (e.g., students can learn the steps described previously and how to apply them to different decisions) or specific to certain types of decisions (e.g., decisions about social activities, taking classes). Both strategies can be useful, and skills can be taught through role-playing, modeling, or prompting. In either approach, promoting generalization across different contexts and decisions is crucial. For students with ASD, who benefit from concrete examples, focusing on decision making in a specific context may be a useful way to begin.

Creating Opportunities for Solving Problems and Making Decisions

Opportunities to solve problems and make decisions, both large and small, come up throughout the school day. Throughout childhood and adolescence, young people must make decisions and solve problems. As students enter late-elementary-age years, they are able to identify problems and problem situations, and this can be a natural time to begin discussing problems and solutions. In younger children, problems with clear solutions are more appropriate targets, but as children age and move into adolescence, more complex problems can be tackled. Building a strong foundation with modeling, role-playing, and creating opportunities for simple decision engagement and problem solving in childhood can set the stage for later applications of complex problem-solving and decision-making experiences. Taking advantage of natural opportunities for solving problems and making decisions is a great way to embed such skill instruction throughout the curriculum and the school day, although a blend of general and content-specific problem-solving and decision-making instruction is likely needed, as specific decision-making and problem-solving skills may be needed in social and in specific academic contexts. Creating opportunities for explicit instruction in the steps described in the previous sections is necessary and will empower students to engage with problems and decisions. Creating opportunities within the school day to review these skills, practice the steps, model and role-play using the steps, and then apply these skills to different situations, is necessary to promote generalization. Providing multiple examples of new concepts, such as uncertainty and risk, increases opportunities for practicing and generalizing these skills across environments.

Across the life span, individualizing instruction in decision making and problem solving based on children's age and support needs becomes necessary. As children learn perspective taking, which typically happens in early childhood but may be delayed in children with ASD, they can begin to identify multiple perspectives on problems and possible solutions. Developing planning skills and being able to identify relevant supports, which also develop throughout childhood, are also important skills to consider. Children might first use some of these skills in playing games and learning to follow classroom and other social rules.

It may also be that students use multiple strategies to solve problems in different situations. For example, social play requires considering different issues and perspectives compared to solving academic problems. Identifying problems that are easier for students to understand or solve can be one way to focus on building on skills that students already have and then focus on generalizing those skills to other situations. Emphasizing the development of perspective taking for students with ASD, particularly in social situations, can enhance problem-solving and decision-making skills. And, as children age, they become better able to generate solutions and evaluate the impact of solutions on outcomes, and therefore able to direct attention to more and more complex decisions and problems. Central to considering complex problems is consequential thinking, which involves understanding the consequences of action, particularly in high-risk situations. Judging risk and assessing probability—and having opportunities to practice these judgment skills in environments that not only offer the chance to take risks and test boundaries but also allow for security and support to learn from the risk taking and boundary testing—can enable children to develop their ability to evaluate possible solutions to problems and make decisions about the best course of action, enhancing their self-determination.

4 Self-Advocacy Skills

For students with ASD, self-advocacy is another skill that can be taught and supported across the life span to enable them to become causal agents in their lives. Having self-advocacy skills is important across multiple domains of life, and requires choice-making, decision-making, and problem-solving skills, as described in previous chapters. Self-advocacy involves having self-understanding and developing the skills necessary to stand up and speak up for yourself and others on behalf of causes you believe in and care about. All students can be self-advocates, with appropriate supports aligned with their support needs. Students who require extensive communication supports can, for example, learn to use their communication supports to share their wants and needs. Ensuring that communication systems are set up to enable self-advocacy will be important across the life span. As students gain self-advocacy skills, they become better able to take on leadership roles and to manage their own learning and behavior, other skills associated with self-determination that are described in later chapters.

Teaching Self-Advocacy Skills

Test, Fowler, Wood, Brewer, and Eddy (2005) identified four key components of self-advocacy, each of which can be explicitly taught across the life span:

1. Knowledge of self
2. Knowledge of rights
3. Communication of one's knowledge of self and rights
4. Leadership

Developing self-knowledge and knowledge of their rights as members of a school, community, and/or society are necessary initial steps for students to be able to communicate such knowledge. Students can then evolve into taking on leadership roles and activities. Identification of one's preferences is an important element of developing self-knowledge, as was discussed in Chapter 2 regarding strategies to support students in identifying their preferences. As students more consistently and accurately identify and communicate their preferences, they learn more about themselves and become better able to express these preferences, verbally and nonverbally, to others. When teaching self-advocacy skills, considering ways to continue to expose students with ASD to diverse situations and experiences so that they can learn more about themselves, their general preferences, and their unique learning needs and preferences helps enable the growth of self-knowledge.

Knowing about oneself is more than just understanding your preferences, however. It also involves understanding your strengths and areas in which supports are needed. Part of understanding one's strengths and needed supports involves understanding support needs arising from one's disability. Helping students with ASD understand their unique profile of strengths and needs will enable them to have a better self-understanding. This can involve discussions about ASD, incorporation of content related to ASD and people with autism in the curriculum, and other strategies to create opportunities for understanding ASD. This can also involve identifying the unique strengths and areas of supports needed that ASD results in for each person. Such instruction should be linked to the diversity of support needs that each student has, regardless of whether he or she has ASD. Students can list their strengths and the areas in which they need support. After students identify these areas, they can begin to identify how they can use their strengths and identify and receive the supports that they need.

One strategy for promoting communication and students' self-understanding as well is to support students with ASD to create PowerPoint presentations that highlight their strengths, their needed supports, and their goals for the future. The complexity of such a presentation can be increased over time, but, even in elementary school, pictures and other tools can be used to communicate knowledge, and students can begin to take on learning and communication activities related to their strengths and preferences. As students develop, such skills can lead to leadership opportunities and can create an understanding that can be used to advocate for their needs throughout their schooling and post-school life. For example, students can present this information about themselves at IEP and educational planning meetings. Some schools have used this approach not only during IEP meetings but also during parent–teacher conferences for all students (i.e., not just students with disabilities), to empower students to identify their strengths and needs and communicate these to their family and teachers, and to better understand themselves. For children with ASD, considering preferences and needed supports related to social interactions and communication may be particularly important. Embedding elements of self-advocacy instruction into social skills instruction and supports can enable students to better understand what they need and how to access it in their environment. Additionally, students who have difficulty in relation to abstract concepts may need more supports with self-advocacy and the communication required to express preferences and needs.

Systematically planning for the integration of these concepts into interventions to enhance social skills and communication can lead to positive outcomes in both domains.

In addition to understanding the personal and disability-related supports they require, students with ASD also need to learn about their rights related to disability accommodations and supports, as well more general rights and responsibilities as a citizen and community member (e.g., voting, participating in community activities). Creating opportunities to learn about (a) the history of the disability rights movement, (b) leaders with ASD, (c) reasonable accommodations under the Americans with Disabilities Act related to employment and postsecondary education, and (d) rights under the Individuals with Disabilities Education Act is an important first step. This instruction can be integrated into government and related social science classes, as well as instruction related to educational planning and involvement in the IEP meeting. Older students can also participate in mock interviews and other situations where they can practice (a) describing their strengths and needed supports and (b) requesting accommodations for college and employment situations. Videotaping such mock interviews and using this as a concrete learning tool can also enable students to understand and identify effective ways to communicate their rights. Explicit instruction in rights and responsibilities can help enhance communication skills, although again issues related to complex and abstract concepts must be made clear for learners with ASD. Visual tools and supports can also be helpful. Teachers have created cards that students can keep in their wallets or course binders that list their accommodations and/or support needs. These cards can be used as a tool to help students remember their rights and communicate to others. The steps in requesting accommodations or asking for supports can be printed on such cards, so that students will have access to the information and know how to use it.

Researchers have identified key elements that should be a part of communication training when the focus is on supporting self-advocacy, including

- Body language,
- Listening skills,
- Recruiting help, and
- Assertiveness training (Test et al., 2005).

A key part of enhancing communication skills related to advocacy involves teaching assertive communication skills and differentiating this from aggressive communication. Assertive communication involves being able to identify what you want and have the confidence to express openly and honestly what that is. This can occur verbally or with other communication supports. Assertive communication may also involve negotiation, particularly when various parties have to compromise. A focus on understanding and respecting others' positions can be critical, particularly for young people with ASD. Beginning with role-play and video-based examples and progressively moving towards real-world situations is an effective way to create opportunities to develop this focus and related self-advocacy skills. Perspective taking can also be infused throughout the instructional day, across activities, and across communication partners. Effective communication skills training can be a part of picking classes, communicating with teachers about support needs, and participating in IEP and transition meetings, as well as negotiating social activities, working in groups in classes, and making decisions within groups. To learn these skills, students will need varying supports, but even students who use extensive communication supports can learn and communicate about their instructional, social, and other needs. Using video portfolios, video-modeling or self-modeling, or other technology-based tools can enable all students to communicate about themselves and their needs both to family members and other support professionals, as well as to peers and friends.

Finally, creating opportunities for students to take on increasing leadership roles in classroom activities can enable them to use their growing knowledge and communication skills. This can involve students taking on leadership roles in class sessions and group activities, extracurricular activities, and other school-related activities. As students take on these opportunities, they build more knowledge of themselves and their needed supports, and further develop communication and leadership skills.

Creating Opportunities for Self-Advocacy

The Individuals with Disabilities Education Act requires that students be invited to their IEP meetings when transition is being discussed. This requirement is mandated for students with disabilities who are age 16 and over (although some states require this to occur at an earlier age). Participation in the IEP meeting creates natural opportunities for students with ASD to learn more about themselves, their strengths, supports needed, and goals for the future. However, research has found that students with ASD are less likely than students with other disabilities to attend their IEP meeting (Shogren & Plotner, 2012). Research has also determined that when students with disabilities do attend IEP meetings, they tend to talk very little (Martin, Huber Marshall, & Sale, 2004). But, communicating and taking on leadership roles in educational planning have been linked to positive outcomes for students with disabilities, including students with ASD (Williams-Diehm, Wehmeyer, Palmer, Soukup, & Garner, 2008). And, when students are present, it is more likely that a student's strengths, needs, and interests will be discussed. Students can learn to use their self-advocacy skills while communicating their preferences and interests and participating in generating IEP goals and objectives. This can be a natural opportunity to use PowerPoint presentations as described previously and to practice assertive communication.

Several curricula have also been developed to teach students, including students with ASD, to take on leadership roles in their IEP meetings and transition planning. Two such curricula, the *Self-Directed IEP* (Martin & Marshall, 1995) and *Whose Future Is It Anyway?* (Wehmeyer et al., 2004), have been evaluated and shown to be effective for students with a range of disabilities, including students with ASD. The *Self-Directed IEP* curriculum explicitly teaches students the leadership skills needed to participate in their IEP meetings. The meeting steps taught in the curriculum are provided in Table 4.1. The *Self-Directed IEP* is part of a larger set of lesson units, called the *ChoiceMaker Self-Determination Curriculum* (available free online at https://www.ou.edu/content/education/centers-and-partnerships/zarrow/choicemaker-curriculum.html). This also includes lessons on identifying interests, skills, limits, and goals that can aid students in developing a greater understanding of themselves, their education and postsecondary goals, and the support they need to be successful. The meeting leadership steps listed in Table 4.1 can be explicitly taught, and students can take on one or all of the steps. Because IEP and transition planning happens on a regular basis throughout a student's educational experience, if this process is started early, students can add additional leadership opportunities over time. Also, working with students to identify how the leadership skills in the IEP meeting generalize to other activities (e.g., interviewing for jobs, colleges, internships) will be important, because other meetings, particularly after students transition from school to the adult world, will look very different. Making concrete the skills that can be generalized to other situations can be useful for students with ASD.

Table 4.1. IEP Meeting Steps From the *Self-Directed IEP*

1. Introduce self and team members.
2. State purpose of meeting.
3. Review past goals and progress (including transition goals).
4. Ask for feedback.
5. Ask questions; deal with differences of opinion.
6. State needed supports.
7. Express interests.
8. Express skills and limitations.
9. Expression options and goals.
10. Close meeting by thanking everyone.

Whose Future Is It Anyway? consists of 36 sessions leading to students' ability to self-direct instruction and learn about (a) self- and disability-awareness; (b) making decisions about transition-related outcomes; (c) identifying and securing community resources to support transition services; (d) writing and evaluating transition goals and objectives; (e) communicating effectively in small groups; and (f) developing skills to become an effective team member, leader, or self-advocate. The materials were specifically developed for students to be the end user; that is, they were written for the student to read and directly engage with the content. Students may need varying levels of support, ranging from having the material read aloud or recorded to having steps explained. However, researchers have found that students with a range of support needs can engage with the curriculum and make gains in self-determination and transition knowledge and skills. *Whose Future Is It Anyway?* includes a student workbook and a coach's guide that can be used by teachers to support students in working through the lessons (and is available free online at https://www.ou.edu/content/education/centers-and-partnerships/zarrow/trasition-education-materials/whos-future-is-it-anyway.html). Students who engage with *Whose Future Is it Anyway?* have been found to show increased self-determination and transition knowledge, which can lead to more effective engagement and leadership in transition-planning activities. A key part of *Whose Future Is it Anyway?* involves helping students think about activities after they leave high school and to begin to make these connections. However, starting this process early (e.g., in middle and early high school), enables students and their families to learn more about what resources are available. Additionally, this creates opportunities to examine how preferences and interests change over time and ensure that educational and transition planning reflects students' current interests, preferences, and knowledge of themselves.

Evaluating Self-Advocacy Skills

Evaluating students' self-advocacy skills is a critical element of determining the types of instruction and support that will enable them to grow and develop in their knowledge of themselves, their rights and their ability to communicate about these rights, and their leadership skills. Curriculum-based assessments are suitable for this purpose; for example, the *Self-Directed IEP* includes a criterion-referenced assessment tool that can be used to measure students' learning related to the IEP leadership skills. Observational data can also be collected on students' engagement in IEP meetings and other educational-planning activities. For example, are students communicating more often in meetings after instruction? When information on disability rights and disability-related accommodations is included as part of the curriculum, this can be tested through various classroom assignments. Students can be observed to determine whether they are able to advocate for needed accommodations or supports in classes and in social situations.

Conversations with students can also be a helpful tool to identify the degree to which they can identify preferences and support needs. Discussions of terms like *self-advocacy* and *supports* provide information on what students know as well as insight into ways to link more complex constructs to better understood constructs. For students who need communication supports, examining the best pictures, technology, or other means of self-expression to determine the most effective means of expression can be a useful tool to enhance self-advocacy and, ultimately, self-determination.

5 Goal-Setting and Goal-Attainment Skills

As we described in the Introduction, being self-determined is about engaging in actions that are directed toward being the causal agent in one's life and achieving one's goals. Using the skills discussed in the previous chapters—choice making, decision making, problem solving, and self-advocacy—enables people with and without ASD to make progress toward goals they are working on, make choices and decisions about the goals to prioritize, solve problems encountered in working toward simple and complex goals, and advocate to create opportunities to work toward goals.

Therefore, goals are central to the development of self-determination. Research has described goals as serving the purpose of directing "attention, effort, and action toward goal-relevant actions, at the expense of non-relevant actions" (Locke & Latham, 2006, p. 265). Essentially, goals help us identify what we are working toward; keep us focused; and enable us to make decisions, regulate our behavior, and prioritize actions that move us forward. Research has consistently found that when people set goals across academic, social, employment, and recreation/leisure domains, they make more progress than if there are no goals set to direct action. And, when students are involved in setting their own goals, they can have a clear and consistent objective that they are working toward, helping them break down complex situations and identify and implement action plans for achieving their goals.

Teaching Goal Setting and Attainment

There are, generally, four steps in the goal-setting and goal-attainment process:

1. Identifying a goal,
2. Defining a goal clearly and concretely,
3. Specifying the actions necessary to achieve the desired outcome, and
4. Evaluating progress and adjusting plan or goal as needed (Wehmeyer et al., 2007).

Students can identify goals in multiple ways. For some students, brainstorming with planning teams, friends, and family members can help identify goal possibilities. For other students, particularly in academic areas, being offered choices between different targets in a class or the curriculum can be a meaningful place to start and a way to practice choice-making skills and using self-knowledge to choose appropriate goals. Other students might already have goals they are considering. Experiences and exposure to how others select goals will help students refine and develop their goal-selection strategies. When first introducing goal selection, starting with domains like recreation and leisure or other domains that are interesting and motivating to students is often useful so that students have experiences that they can build on. Building on students' personal experiences and subsequently expanding students' opportunities to engage in different activities to further inform goal selection enables students to make more effective choices and decisions about what they want to go after in life.

When students first learn to identify goals, they may tend to select broad goals they have limited ability to achieve given their current knowledge, skills, and experiences. This is expected, and creates a natural teaching opportunity. For example, a student might say that he or she wants to earn an A in a class, but have very limited understanding of what it actually takes to earn that grade. Or a student might identify a specific career he or she wants to pursue, for example, being a professional basketball player, but have no idea the requirements or probability of such a career. In these circumstances, it is important to work with students to break down this broad goal into smaller process goals. *Process goals* are smaller, more specific goals that allow a person to work toward (and perhaps ultimately revise) his or her broad goal. Critical at this step is maintaining a focus on students directing their own goal identification. For example, it can be easy for a teacher or support professional to simply state that "being a professional basketball player is not possible—you need a different goal," or that "earning an A is not possible because of your performance up to this point—you should target passing the class." This shifts the goal, however, from being a student-directed one to being teacher or other directed. But, if the student is supported to break the goal down into smaller steps and engage in efforts to take achieve those, this can lead to additional knowledge that the student can use to revise that original broad goal and help keep the goals student directed. For example, a more manageable goal might be to research what it would take to earn an A or to identify one's current grade. The next process goal might be taking action on one of the activities to improve a grade (e.g., do an extra credit project), or it might lead to a revision of the goal to earn a B in class. Similarly, a student could research the characteristics of professional basketball players (e.g., height, statistics, travel schedules) and evaluate whether these career characteristics align with his or her own skills and interests. After learning the answers, the student could then identify other interests related to basketball or possibly a different career path, based on an understanding of how these requirements align with his or her interests, preferences, and abilities.

This example highlights not only the importance of keeping goals student directed but also the distinction between process goals and outcome, or product, goals. Process goals can be thought of as goals related to the steps that it takes to achieve an outcome or create a product. For example, understanding what is required to earn an A in a class is a process goal related to the outcome of earning an A. Process goals focus on the skills and abilities or activities students need to achieve an outcome, and bring the focus to actionable steps in achieving an outcome. Zimmerman and Kitsantas (1999), researchers who have extensively studied process and outcome goals, have found that students who work only on outcome goals tend to show lower skill development, belief in their ability to achieve their goals, and interest in their goals. But, when they break down outcome goals into process goals, they demonstrate more skill development and belief in their ability to achieve goals. So, teaching students the difference between outcome and process goals and focusing on the role of breaking down broad goals into smaller, more readily achievable process goals can help students make more progress, while not limiting their outcome or product goals. This process creates natural learning opportunities and enables students to take more of a role in setting and managing their own goals. The same is true of students who are targeting social or communication skills or who use communication systems. Various goal options can be programmed into a device or communication support so that students can try different options and select which they prefer. The same is true in social situations where students can be involved in identifying elements they like and do not like and in setting goals related to developing strategies to build new skills or target preferred activities.

Breaking goals into smaller, more achievable process goals can be particularly helpful for children and youth with ASD, as research suggests that students with ASD tend to be more sequential in their goal-directed behavior and can have difficulty working on multiple goals simultaneously. Breaking goals into smaller steps, with fewer steps for each process goal, helps students with ASD to more concretely understand the steps they are taking to make progress toward an outcome or product goal. These skills can be generalized across goals and activities.

After students identify a goal and break it down into process and outcome goals, they can then document their goal in some way: writing it, dictating it, depicting it with a picture, and so forth. Documenting makes the goal more concrete and helps the student take additional ownership of the goal. It also creates a natural reminder, or prompt, to work on the goal when the goal depiction is in an accessible and often-seen location. For students with ASD, this can provide a concrete, visual (and/or verbal) reminder of their goals to which they can easily refer.

Next, students can begin to develop an action plan. Action planning involves developing the specific strategies and supports that will be needed to make progress toward a goal. This involves the student discussing and identifying, with guidance and supports, what they know and what they need to need to know about how to make progress toward their goal. Emphasizing the role of supports, including people such as teachers, family, and peers, as well as technology, can be part of these discussions. Students can use the self-regulation strategies—specifically self-monitoring, self-evaluation, and self-reinforcement strategies—discussed in Chapter 6 to take steps toward achieving their goals. As a teacher or support person, you will likely be actively involved in creating these supports and teaching students how to use them in working toward their goals, and helping them take on increased responsibility for these skills over time.

As students implement action plans, another critical step is supporting them to evaluate whether they have achieved their goals. It is important to recognize that setting a goal and implementing an action plan does not always lead to goal attainment. When goals are not attained, this is not a negative outcome, but, instead, a learning opportunity. For example, it may be that the goal needs to be revised or that a different action plan is needed. Thinking through why a goal or action plan needs to be changed creates an opportunity for learning in greater depth about one's strengths, interests, and supports needed in relation to goal setting and action planning, and the process promotes self-regulation opportunities, as students can learn about how to make adjustments to their actions to make progress toward goals. Ongoing discussion about goal revision is important and highlights how this process is a dynamic one, used by all people to continuously work toward their goals. This also highlights the importance of supporting students to recognize that goal setting is a continuous process. That is, if a goal is not achieved, revision to the goal itself or the action plan is needed, and then work toward the goal can continue. And if a goal is achieved, this is a prompt to think about the next goal in the goal sequence. For example, if a student has identified what it takes to earn a certain grade in a class, the next goal might be to develop a plan for addressing those requirements.

Creating Opportunities for Goal Setting and Attainment

Goal-setting activities can be incorporated into a variety of educational activities and instructional areas, across the life span. To promote goal setting for an adolescent with ASD, Held, Thoma, and Thomas (2004) developed a multicomponent intervention incorporating several approaches, including implementing the Self-Determined Learning Model of Instruction (which is described in detail in Chapter 8), to assist the student in setting goals in his or her personal life (including social interactions), school work, and post-school outcomes. Overall, research has consistently shown that students perform better when they are working toward goals, suggesting the value of creating opportunities for goal setting not only for promoting self-determination but also for enhancing student performance and goal attainment. However, there are several important things to consider when working on creating opportunities for students to set and attain goals.

First, students should have the needed skills (or be provided adequate supports) to make progress toward their goals. If students are interested in goals that they do not currently have the skills to attain, this can be an opportunity to break the goal down and identify the steps that need to be taken to develop those skills and identify necessary supports. This is where a teacher or support person can play a key role through modeling, role-play, and explicit instruction. However, retaining a focus on supporting students to identify and understand the steps they are taking to break down the goal and develop an action plan promotes the development of student self-direction and self-determination. A way that this can be approached in the education context is to work with students to define process goals for their day-to-day work, and remind them of their outcome goals to help facilitate motivation and a long-term perspective on the purpose of their process goals.

However, while it is important that students have the skills to make progress toward their goals, the goals still need to be challenging. Research has found that challenging goals lead to greater levels of performance than do easy or vague goals, perhaps because such goals require students to push themselves to move forward and motivate them to act (Locke & Latham, 2006). One of the benefits of challenging goals is that they create a discrepancy between the current state and a desired future state. If there is not a goal, there is also not a focus on what actions need to be taken to move forward. Goals that are associated with high expectations and that challenge students can enhance students' motivation.

Motivation is a key part of goal-directed action. This means that another important consideration is ensuring that goals are aligned with student's preferences, interests, and goals for themselves. Considering what students know and express about their preferences and interests can help identify goals. Making sure that goals are developed not only on school-based expectations but also on student and family interests, preferences, and values is important. This is why, in the context of transition planning, such a strong emphasis is placed on ensuring that students' interests and preferences guide the process. Researchers have found that there is often a misalignment of transition goals with student interests and preferences, particularly for students from diverse backgrounds (Trainor, 2005). For example, goals often overemphasize independence rather than interdependence in community living and adulthood. This suggests the need, over the life span, to ensure that students with ASD and their families are engaged in conversations about their goals for the future and that these outcome goals are used to shape process goals throughout life.

6 Self-Regulation and Self-Management Skills

Acting in a self-determined manner requires that children and youth with ASD have the skills to self-direct their actions as they work toward goals. Managing and self-directing one's actions is part of self-regulation, which is the process of

- Making decisions about how to act,
- Evaluating the desirability of possible outcomes, and
- Reviewing action plans and revising as necessary based on an understanding of the context and its demands (Whitman, 1990).

Teaching students self-regulated learning strategies gives them the skills to know how to prompt, monitor, and evaluate their behavior, which enables them to self-direct their actions and become more self-determined.

Research has established that student-directed learning strategies have benefits for students across their school careers. For example, Lee, Simpson, and Shogren (2007) reviewed the literature on self-management strategies for students with ASD and found benefits across multiple domains. Researchers have also found that student-directed strategies can reduce the demands on teachers to manage students' behavior. For example, one study that compared student-directed and teacher-directed strategies for elementary school students with ASD found that both were successful in improving students' classroom behavior and engagement in classroom activities related to math, science, and literacy. However, the classroom teacher said, "If the children do it themselves, it is much easier" (Shogren, Lang, Machalicek, Rispoli, & O'Reilly, 2011, p. 94). She elaborated by saying that when students were self-managing their behavior, she did not have to watch every student and try to stay on track with acknowledging and reinforcing each good behavior; instead, the students learned what good behavior was and how to reinforce themselves.

Teaching Self-Regulation and Self-Management Skills

There are four common student-directed learning strategies that enable students to begin to self-regulate and self-manage their actions and behavior: antecedent cue regulation, self-monitoring, self-evaluation, and self-reinforcement. The first strategy, antecedent cue regulation, is a strategy focused on providing prompts before and/or during a task or activity to enable a person to understand how to complete that task or activity. The remaining strategies are consequent strategies that are used after an action is performed and involve monitoring performance (self-monitoring), evaluating performance (self-evaluation) and reinforcing performance (self-reinforcement).

Antecedent Cue Regulation

Antecedent cue regulation has been used extensively with students with disabilities, including children and youth with ASD. *Antecedent cue regulation* involves the use of picture, audio, or even written prompts to guide completion of a task or activity. This can range from simple and widely used strategies, such as to-do lists or GPS navigation systems, to more complex technologies, like self-prompting systems designed to run on tablet PCs or iPads or iPhones.

To create effective antecedent cues, the first step is determining the task or activity the student needs support to learn to complete. Antecedent cues can be used to teach new skills or to guide students in completing complex tasks that they would struggle to complete without support. For example, antecedent cue strategies have been used to promote social interactions by providing a step-by-step script or a series of prompts that a student can use to engage and invite others to participate in social activities. After selecting a task or activity, several additional issues need to be considered:

- What level of detail is needed in the cue(s)?
- What type of prompt works best for the student (e.g., visual, auditory, written)?
- What is the best cuing and prompting format?
- What is the best delivery mechanism?

To determine the level of detail needed, tasks or activities can be task-analyzed (broken down into steps), and then the level of detail in the cue(s) needed by each student can be individualized. For example, some students might require that cues for every step be provided, while other students may need only certain steps in the routine to be highlighted. Audio, visual, and pictorial prompts can be evaluated to determine which one is best, and student preferences can be tested. Prompts that promote greater independence should be considered. For example, if audio prompts are preferred and most effective, can these be recorded so that a student can listen to them on headphones, instead of having someone be there to deliver the prompts? Finally, in terms of delivery, think through whether the prompts will be delivered through a prompt book, technology (e.g., smartphone, PC, tablet), audio files, or some other mechanism. Emerging technologies are providing more and more apps that can be used to deliver prompts in an accessible and unobtrusive way. Staying current on emerging technologies and their applications for prompting and using pictures, video, and audio will enable effective use of these strategies.

Antecedent cue regulation strategies can be used to teach social skills (e.g., picture cue books can be developed for social activities, social scripts can be written for activities), to teach transition skills (e.g., various community living skills are very amenable to antecedent cues, such as cooking—a recipe is essentially an antecedent cue strategy—or doing laundry; various employment-related skills, such as specific job tasks or asking for supports or accommodations), to teach academic skills (e.g., breaking down the steps of completing an assignment, doing a math operation), or to promote academic engagement (e.g., antecedent prompts to stay on task). Antecedent cue strategies can be used by all students, although the level of specificity and support will likely be more intense for students with ASD. Further, the types of supports needed may vary across activities and tasks; students might need more prompts in social activities, for example, and fewer in academic activities. Or, students may prefer picture cues for academic engagement and videos for social activities.

Self-Monitoring

Self-monitoring is another self-directed learning strategy that has been extensively researched in students with disabilities, including students with ASD. There are two components of self-monitoring:

1. Self-assessment
2. Self-recording

Students need to understand and use both skills to self-monitor their behavior, and specific teaching strategies exist to teach both skills. Self-assessment involves identifying whether a targeted behavior has occurred (or in some cases, did not occur), and self-recording involves documenting when the behavior occurred (or did not occur). The documentation can involve making checks on a self-monitoring sheet (see Figure 6.1), dropping pennies in a jar, or using technology to document performance. In addition to recording how frequently a behavior occurs (i.e., frequency recording), recording how long the behavior occurs (i.e., duration recording) may also be useful for some behaviors, for example, if the student's goal was to monitor how long he or she stayed engaged in class activities. A student can use a timer on a watch or smartphone to engage in duration recording.

To teach students to self-monitor, there are three broad steps suggested by Agran et al. (2003):

1. Introduce the behavior to be self-monitored, ensuring students can differentiate the occurrence/nonoccurrence of the behavior.
2. Introduce the self-monitoring system by modeling its use and prompting the student to use the system, fading prompts over time.
3. Create opportunities for the student to practice using the self-monitoring system in natural environments.

Matt's Self-Monitoring Checklist

How Well Am I Working?

(student is wearing a vibrating watch that goes off every 5 minutes)

Each time your watch vibrates, give yourself a:

+ for working well

− for not working well

1	2	3	4	5	6	7	8	9	10

Goal for Today: Working Well __8__ time slots

How many time slots was I working well this session? ______

Did I reach my goal for today? ____ Yes ____ No

Figure 6.1. Sample self-monitoring checklist.

There are a couple of additional things to keep in mind when supporting students to develop a self-monitoring system. First, the behavior to be self-monitored has to be easily defined and important to the student. It is also useful to think about behaviors that might have an impact across settings. This also necessitates an evaluation of the student's current performance (or baseline). Self-monitoring is not typically used to teach new behaviors. Instead, it is used to increase performance of behaviors that are already in the student's repertoire. Understanding what is influencing a student's current behavior is important, as this can shape self-monitoring strategies. For example, is a student performing the behavior inconsistently (e.g., only occasionally initiates social interactions) or does he or she perform the behavior at inappropriate times (e.g., interrupting others to ask questions)? Second, do not get overly focused on complete and all-inclusive accuracy in self-monitoring. Research has shown that some errors are expected, and simply becoming more aware of one's performance and actions can lead to changes in behavior. Third, think carefully about how students record their behavior. What is an unobtrusive way that works for them, and how often will they need to self-record? If the focus is on increasing on-task behavior in the classroom, for example, you might set up an interval system (e.g., the student is alerted with a vibrating alarm every 5 minutes to record whether he or she is on task), but if the focus is on social interactions, it may be more infrequent recording, such as every time the student initiates a social interaction with a peer during a free-play activity. You also have to ask yourself, what is the best way to alert the student? Will the student respond better to paper-and-pencil methods or to technology-based supports? How will you support the student to recognize that self-monitoring and self-recording needs to occur, particularly in situations where the behavior may occur infrequently?

After making these decisions, you can then teach the student to use the self-monitoring system. To do this, you can role-play use of the system, record videos of the student or peers using the system, and so forth. Each of these components helps students develop the skills they need to assess their performance of the behavior and record it.

Self-monitoring systems can be targeted to individual students or to groups of students. For example, self-monitoring systems can be used with a class, with all students recording their achievement of a learning goal daily or weekly on a chalkboard or smartboard. Then, students can encourage each other to achieve their goals, and the class can earn rewards when all students achieve their goals. Research has found that self-monitoring can impact academic engagement as well as increase academic skills for individual students and for groups of students. For individual students with ASD, self-monitoring has been shown to increase the use of social skills and other desired behavioral outcomes.

Self-Evaluation

After students have learned and are routinely implementing self-monitoring strategies, the next two strategies—self-evaluation and self-reinforcement—can be added to self-monitoring systems. Self-evaluation is an extension of self-monitoring. It involves evaluating the quality of the targeted behavior, as informed by information collected through the self-monitoring process, in comparison to a standard (as set by the goal). For example, did the student stay on task for 80% of intervals? Did he or she initiate social interactions two times in a day? A key part of self-evaluation is making the standard clear, linking it to the goal, and setting it ahead of time. This provides not only clear expectations for the student but also a target to work toward. Figure 6.1 includes self-evaluation in a self-monitoring sheet. The target number for the day is identified, and the student indicates whether he or she has met this target. A key aspect of teaching self-evaluation skills is that enabling students to evaluate themselves reduces their dependence on others for feedback and enables them to respond to the demands and expectations of the environment. Students can, over time, be involved in setting expectations for themselves as they learn what behavior is expected in the classroom, in other activities, and in social activities.

While self-evaluation is linked to self-monitoring, teaching self-evaluation requires additional instruction so that students can understand and apply the criteria set by the student or the teacher or jointly. To teach self-evaluation skills, Agran and colleagues (2003) suggested steps similar to teaching self-monitoring, with the addition of evaluation strategies:

1. Select the target behavior or activity AND evaluation criteria.
2. Provide a rationale that is understandable to the student for why the behavior is important.
3. Provide opportunities to practice the behavior and use the evaluation criteria.
4. Introduce the evaluation system and materials.
   - Match the system to the context and student's abilities.
5. Have a teacher or peer model use the system while performing the behavior.
6. Support the student to practice using the system by
   - Guided practice
   - Role-play
   - Natural situation practice
   - Independent practice
7. Fade assistance and enable the student to perform the behavior in natural environments.

A key element here is the addition of instruction on the self-evaluation criteria. As with self-monitoring, students can watch videos of themselves or peers in the targeted context, evaluating whether the target behavior occurred and adding the additional step of evaluating the behavior across the observation.

Both research and anecdotal teacher reports have established that adding self-evaluation to self-monitoring can promote increased academic, social, and transition-related skills. Self-evaluation activities also create natural opportunities for learning and application of math skills (e.g., counting number of times a behavior was preformed, calculating percentages) and can be used to learn graphing and other skills so that students can see and document changes in their behavior over time. Even if students do not construct graphs or charts themselves, viewing these visual depictions can provide learning opportunities related to using information to make decisions. Think carefully about the individualized supports that will make the self-monitoring and self-evaluation system most relevant and useful for the student. As with all other strategies, think about how technology-based, visual, and other types of supports can be maximized to promote meaningful student engagement.

Self-Reinforcement

Finally, one additional student-directed strategy that can be useful to consider is self-reinforcement. As is the case with the self-monitoring and self-evaluation processes, to self-reinforce, students have to learn to identify whether they have performed a target behavior. Self-reinforcement adds the additional element of students delivering reinforcement to themselves based on their evaluation of the performance of the behavior or activity. Reinforcers may be the same that a teacher or other person would deliver (e.g., praise, access to another preferred activity). The difference is that students are gaining control over not only monitoring and evaluating their behavior but also reinforcing that behavior. This can enhance self-regulation, particularly as students may begin to develop a greater understanding of the relationship between their actions and the outcomes they experience.

Students should, to the maximum degree possible, be involved in selecting the reinforcers they will deliver to themselves to further enhance motivation. Self-reinforcement can be used alone (i.e., students deliver a reinforcer to themselves contingent on the occurrence of the behavior), in combination with self-monitoring (i.e., students deliver a reinforcer to themselves after recording the occurrence of the behavior), or in combination with self-monitoring and evaluation (i.e., students deliver a reinforcer to themselves after recording the occurrence of a behavior and determining that a standard was met for the performance of the behavior). It often makes sense to begin with self-monitoring, add self-evaluation, and then use self-reinforcement.

An easy way to begin teaching students about self-reinforcement is to focus on the contingency:

- If _______________, then _______________.
- An example for a younger student might be, **IF** I complete my assigned morning calendar work, **THEN** I give myself a pat on the back and put an animal sticker on my daily self-record chart.
- Or for an older student, **IF** I complete all the tasks at my job site, **THEN** I will earn a paycheck that I can use to buy a new video game.

Students can fill in the behavior or activity they are targeting (and they can do this in writing, verbally, with pictures, or using technology) and then the reinforcer they wish to self-administer.

It is also important to consider that reinforcers do not have to be something that is immediately delivered, although it can be useful to start this way. A reinforcer could be doing something that the student enjoys in the evening, like having a meal at a favorite restaurant (although make sure this is communicated with family members and other stakeholders) after completing so many instances of a behavior or after having a week of achieving a target for on-task behavior in the classroom. Over time, the number of performances or the accuracy of performance can be increased, making self-reinforcement dependent on higher and higher expectations. For example, a student might go from reinforcing him- or herself for initiating any social interaction to reinforcing after initiating five social interactions. And, eventually, the social interactions and resulting outcomes may become reinforcing on their own, or the reinforcers will become tied to real-life consequences (e.g., earning a good grade, earning money for work completed).

Like all consequent strategies, the target behavior and expectations need to be matched to students' interests, needs, and current abilities. The reinforcer also has to be something motivating so that when the student delivers it to him- or herself, it leads to increases in desired behaviors. Additionally, research has found that students can learn to deliver their own reinforcers, do so accurately, and that this can lead to increases in behavior above and beyond the increases seen when teachers deliver reinforcement.

Creating Opportunities for Self-Regulation and Self-Management

Student-directed strategies can be applied to a number of different tasks and activities, and strategies can be used alone or in combination to create meaningful student outcomes. For some students it might make sense to start with antecedent strategies to build capacity and activities that the student can self-monitor, self-evaluate, and self-reinforce. It is important for consequent strategies that these are skills that the student can already perform, but are not being used consistently or appropriately. However, antecedent strategies can be used to teach new skills while at the same time using consequent strategies to increase the use of existing behaviors. Overall, the more that students are engaged in directing their own learning and behavior with individualized supports that enable them to use these strategies effectively, the greater the impacts on motivation, behavior, and resulting self-determination. Continuously evaluating the effectiveness and appropriateness of existing self-regulation supports (i.e., evaluating whether the student is showing increases in performance of the target behavior as well as use of the strategies) will help enhance the outcomes that students experience, because these supports and the behaviors, activities, reinforcers, and criteria for evaluation necessarily change over time, with age, and with new and different environmental demands.

7 Self-Awareness and Self-Knowledge

Each of the previous chapters has focused on teaching specific skills—choice making, decision making and problem solving, self-advocacy, goal setting and attainment, and self-regulation and self-management. This chapter focuses on slightly different, yet still important, issues related to promoting and enhancing self-determination—building student self-awareness and self-knowledge. Self-awareness and self-knowledge are foundational to one's ability to act in a self-determined manner, particularly to make effective choices and decisions, to set personally meaningful goals, and to advocate for things that are important. They also play a key role in all of the skills discussed previously. For example, self-awareness and self-knowledge relate to making choices, communicating about oneself, selecting goals, and so on.

As such, self-awareness and self-knowledge develops over time and with experience with each of the previous skill areas. Additionally, however, aspects of self-awareness and self-knowledge can be taught, often in conjunction with skills described in previous chapters. Another key element of building student self-awareness and self-knowledge is creating opportunities for students to see the relationship between actions based on their self-awareness and self-knowledge and the outcomes they experience. This enables students to develop beliefs about themselves and how their actions influence their environment. Terms like *empowerment* are often used to describe students who recognize that their actions can have an impact on their environments and the outcomes they experience. Historically, students with disabilities often have had restricted opportunities to make choices, to set goals, and to direct their own learning. In this scenario, students may have tried to engage in actions to affect their environment, but learned that those actions did not influence their environment in the expected ways. Students who have these experiences sometimes become disempowered, relying on others to make things happen for them, or they begin to engage in actions that are deemed to be problematic in order to express that they want things in their environment, because such behaviors often receive more attention and have a greater impact on the environment. Thus, a critical aspect of promoting self-determination is ensuring that students come to recognize the relationship between their actions that are based on knowledge and awareness of themselves and the outcomes they experience. Engagement in skills teaching alone does not result in the development of self-determination; it is also facilitated by development of these action-control beliefs.

Promoting Self-Awareness and Self-Knowledge

People who are self-aware and have self-knowledge possess a reasonably accurate understanding of their strengths, abilities, unique learning/support needs, and limitations. And, they are able to use this knowledge to engage in self-determined actions to get the things they need to be successful and make progress on goals. Researchers, teachers, and other practitioners have developed approaches that students with ASD can use to develop a greater understanding of the autism spectrum and how having ASD affects their lives, as well as their unique strengths and supports needed. One particular approach includes a workbook that has activities prompting students to: (a) think about their strengths and abilities; (b) reflect on how they best learn; (c) understand their sensory experiences, abilities, and social/communication skills; and (d) identify why they sometimes feel upset. It also guides students to identify the significant people in their lives and how they can use them to build self-awareness and the supports needed to be successful (Faherty, 2000).

Chang, Durham, and Little (in press) identified several strategies that teachers can use to enable students to feel more autonomous and competent in classrooms, promoting their action-control beliefs as well as greater self-knowledge and self-awareness. They suggested that teachers consider:

1. *Frequently communicating expectations and checking in to ensure students understand expectations.* Teachers can also discuss students' perceptions of their abilities in relation to expectations and articulate situations where actions affect outcomes (both positively and negatively), making students more aware of the relationship between actions and outcomes.
2. *Offering choices throughout instructional activities and removing controlling events.* Involve students, whenever possible, in selecting and designing assignments and learning activities and in participating in grading and the like can promote greater action-control beliefs, as students can learn to understand the relationship between their actions and outcomes. This can be a natural opportunity to focus on problem solving and decision making as well as building self-awareness and self-knowledge.

3. *Enabling students to actively participate in the classroom.* Similar to the previous steps, teachers can consider ways to promote active student engagement based on student identification of the ways they most effectively learn. Consider the use of activities that help students better understand the ways that they learn best so that they can use this self-awareness and self-knowledge to participate in class activities and maximize their learning opportunities.
4. *Providing positive and informational feedback.* Research has shown that students benefit from feedback that is not only positive but also directly linked to actions they have taken. For example, rather than telling a student that he or she is smart, praise the student's effort on a specific task. This can be a more effective way to increase self-awareness and self-knowledge. As students receive concrete examples of the skills they are effective at and learn how using these skills can affect outcomes, they gain both self-confidence and competence.
5. *Providing structured guidance.* When teachers focus on creating environments that support autonomy, this does not mean that students will no longer need guidance and support. Rather, the nature of that guidance and support changes to promote students' self-direction of learning and greater self-awareness of the effects of their actions. This changes the teacher's role from one of director to facilitator. This subtle shift helps students help themselves, and when teachers facilitate clear expectations, action planning, and instructional feedback, a meaningful structure can be created in the classroom that enables students' self-determination. Structured guidance promoting self-direction and self-awareness is particularly useful for students with ASD, because this classroom atmosphere promotes greater clarity in expectations and provides students with the opportunity to discuss strengths and support needs on a routine basis, which helps them make connections between actions and outcomes.

For children and youth with ASD, considering strategies that build empowerment, enable the identification and expression of self-knowledge, and provide explicit links between action and outcomes is important across the life span. Efforts should begin in young children, with activities such as labeling emotions and feelings and recognizing that different people have different preferences, and should include informational feedback on task performance. As children mature, they become better able to evaluate their own performance. This is a natural time (later elementary to early-secondary years, typically) to begin focusing on self-evaluation skills, linking knowledge of actions taken with outcomes.

This can also be a time when self-advocacy skills related to requesting help and supports can be targeted, as students gain more understanding of areas where they struggle to achieve valued outcomes. Overall, modeling and having ongoing conversations about actions and outcomes is a way to help students understand the consequences of actions and recognize that their actions influence outcomes in a supportive environment, leading to enhanced self-determination.

8 The Self-Determined Learning Model of Instruction

The previous chapters discuss specific skills and attitudes that can be taught and promoted by educators and others who support children and youth with ASD to enhance skills associated with the development of self-determination. Teaching each of these skills is important, and some research has suggested that using multicomponent interventions that target multiple self-determination skills simultaneously can be a highly effective way to promote the development of self-determination, particularly as so many of the skills are linked (Cobb, Lehmann, Newman-Gonchar, & Alwell, 2009). One such evidence-based, multicomponent intervention to promote self-determination and self-regulated goal setting and attainment is the Self-Determined Learning Model of Instruction (SDLMI; Wehmeyer, Palmer, Agran, Mithaug, & Martin, 2000). The SDLMI is a model of instruction that provides a framework for teachers to use when designing instruction to enable students to self-direct learning and enhance self-determination. The SDLMI specifically focuses on self-regulated problem solving, in service to a goal that the student sets and works toward. The SDLMI creates opportunities for students to focus on choice making, problem solving, decision making, and self-advocacy. Further, working through the SDLMI can enhance self-awareness and self-knowledge.

Implementing the Self-Determined Learning Model of Instruction

Implementation of the SDLMI consists of a three-phase instructional process. Each instructional phase presents a problem to be solved by the student, which the student solves by posing and answering a series of four Student Questions per phase (see Figure 8.1). The goal of instruction is that students learn the questions, make them their own, and apply them to reach self-selected goals. Each student question is also linked to a set of Teacher Objectives that specifically pertains to what the teacher is trying to support each student to achieve in answering the questions. Each instructional phase also includes a list of Educational Supports

(text continues on p. 52)

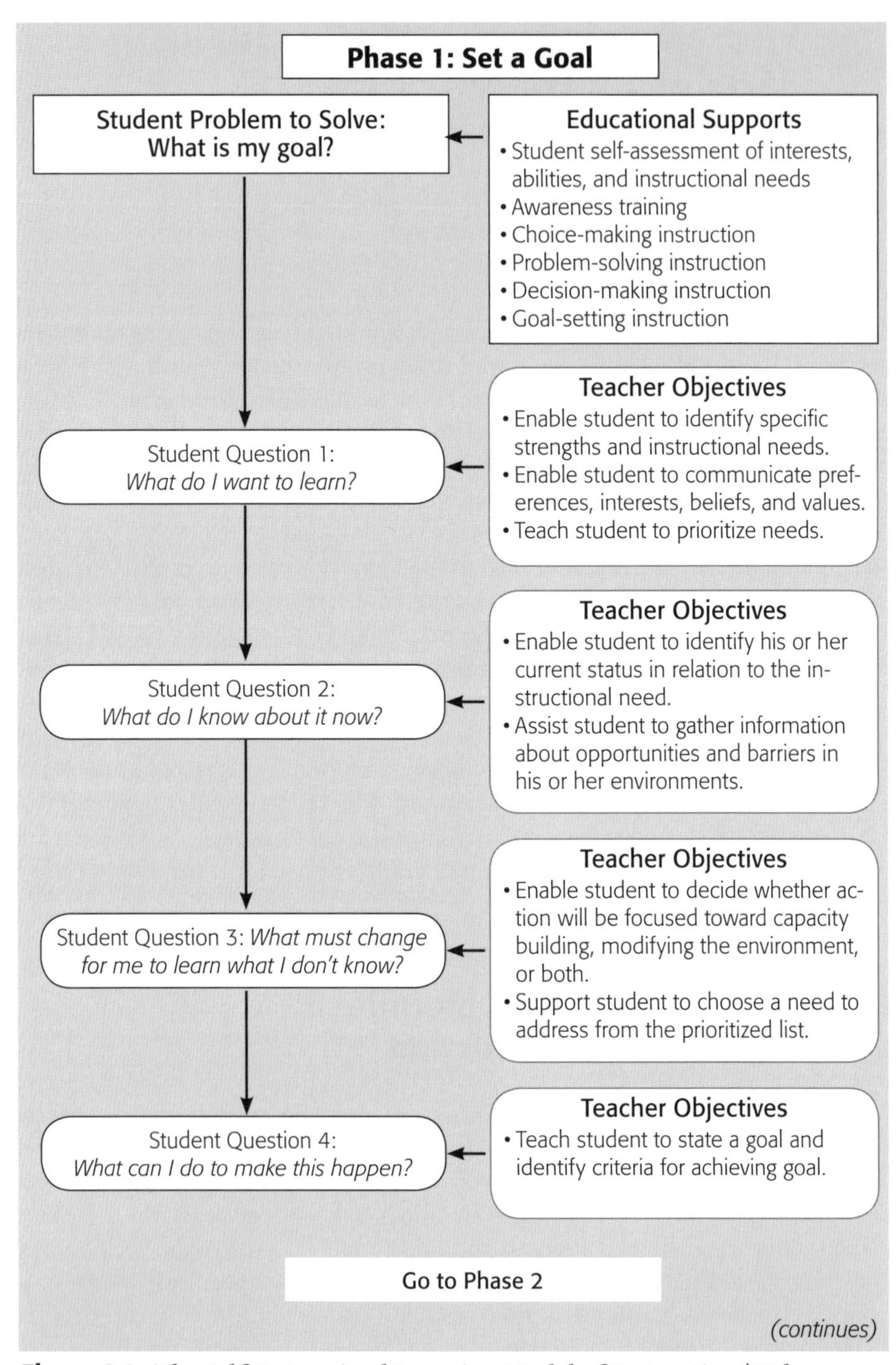

Figure 8.1. The Self-Determined Learning Model of Instruction (Wehmeyer et al., 2003; reprinted with permission).

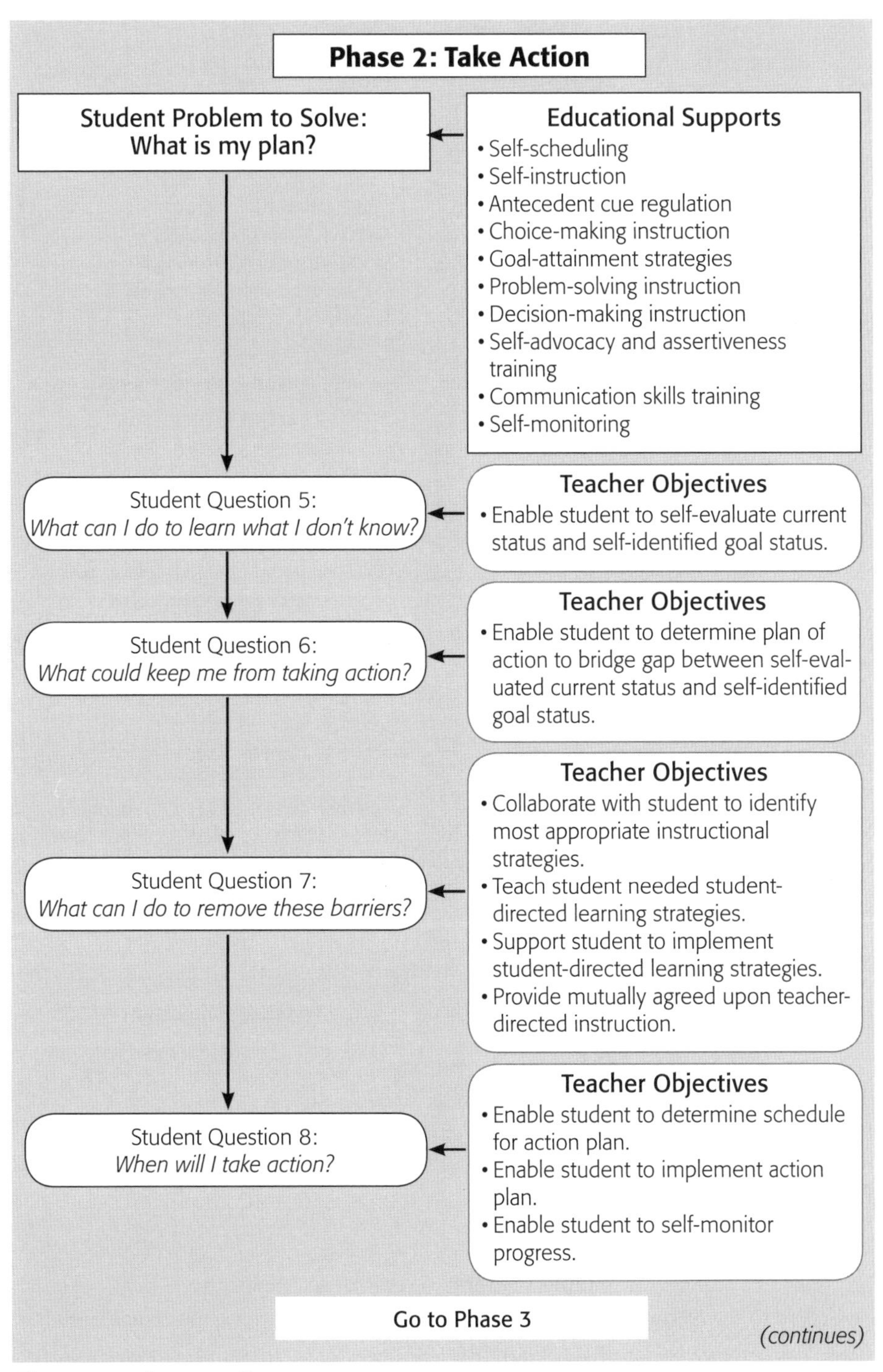

Figure 8.1. *(continued)*

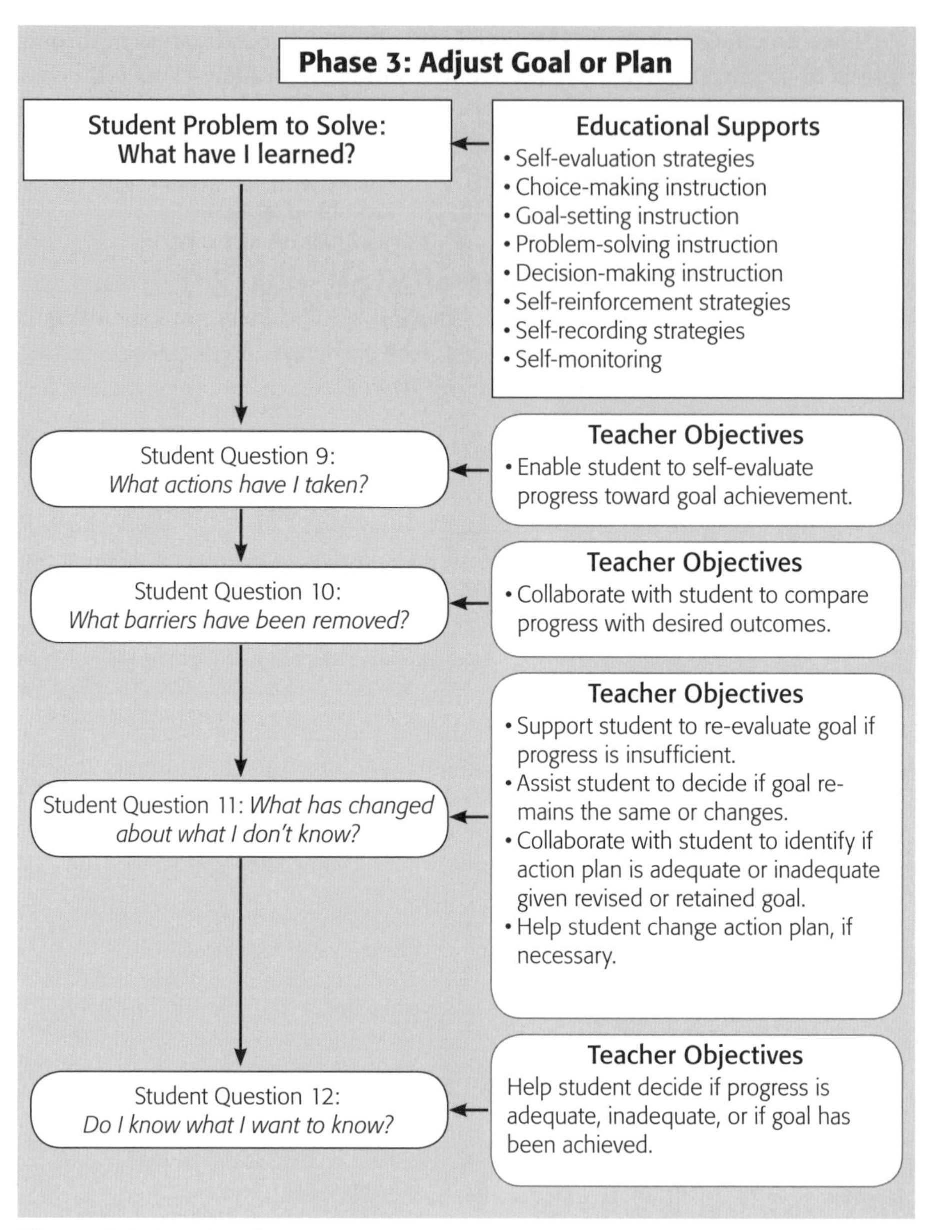

Figure 8.1. (*continued*)

that teachers can use to enable students to self-direct learning. These supports are linked to many of the skills listed in the previous chapters, and teaching strategies described in each of these chapters can be used in the context of teaching students to answer the questions associated with the SDLMI.

The Student Questions in the model are meant to direct the student through a problem-solving sequence in any content domain—academic, social, behavioral, transition. In research studies of the SDLMI with students with disabilities, including students with ASD, students have set academic goals as well as transition, social, and behavioral goals. The SDLMI can be used in any type of class, with supports needed for a range of student characteristics.

As students work through the three phases of the SDLMI (Set a goal, Take action, Adjust goal or plan), they solve the problem posed in each phase, and learn to lead themselves through the phases of the SDLMI. Teachers implementing the model teach students to solve the sequence of problems to construct a means–ends chain—a causal sequence—that moves them from where they are (not having their needs and interests satisfied) to where they want to be (a goal state of having those needs and interests satisfied). Students learn how to self-regulate their actions to reduce or eliminate the discrepancy between what they want or need and what they currently have or know. They also learn how to use multiple skills leading to enhanced self-determination in order to eliminate this discrepancy. It can be helpful for students to use the SDLMI across several activities and content areas so that they get more opportunities to practice this causal sequence. Teachers can create opportunities for instruction using the model in any content domain by embedding the SDLMI instruction in the curriculum, thereby shifting the focus from teachers setting the goals for learning to students setting the goals and teachers sharing the content and opportunities for students to work toward those goals.

Each of the three phases has four questions that students work through. The four questions differ from phase to phase, but represent identical steps in the problem-solving sequence. That is, students answering the questions must:

1. Identify the problem,
2. Identify potential solutions to the problem,
3. Identify barriers to solving the problem, and
4. Identify consequences of each possible solution option.

These steps are the fundamental steps in any problem-solving process, and they form the means–end problem-solving sequence represented by the Student Questions in each phase.

Because the model itself is designed for teachers to implement, the language of the Student Questions is intentionally written at a level that will not be understood by every student; nor does the model assume that students have life experiences that enable them to fully answer each question. The questions are written in first-person voice in a relatively simple format and are intended to be the starting point for discussion between the teacher and the student. Some students will learn and use all 12 questions as they are written. Other students will need to have the questions rephrased to be more understandable. Still other students, because of the intensity of their instructional needs, may have the teacher paraphrase the questions for them. Figure 8.2 provides an example of worksheets that could be used to help the students write responses to the SDLMI. However, other formats can be used to communicate the questions and to help students respond. For example, some teachers have created pictorial versions based on the picture-based systems students use routinely in the classroom. It is important to note that it is not assumed that students already have the skills to effectively answer each of the questions in Figure 8.2. Indeed, the SDLMI provides a framework within which students can learn those skills in the context of self-directed learning.

The first time a teacher uses the model with a student or a group of students, the initial step in the implementation process is to read the question with or to the student, discuss what the question means, and then, if necessary, change the wording to help that student better understand the intent of the question. Such wording changes must, however, be made such that the problem-solving intent of the question remains intact. For example, changing Student Question 1 from "What do I want to learn?" to "What is my goal?" changes the nature of the question. The Teacher Objectives associated with each student question provide direction for teachers regarding the intent of the questions. More appropriate alternatives might be:

- What am I interested in?
- What do I want to learn in science class?

The objectives are what the teacher will be trying to accomplish by implementing the model. In each instructional phase, the objectives are linked directly to the Student Questions. These objectives can be met by using strategies provided in the Educational Supports section of the model. The Teacher Objectives provide teachers with specific objectives that enable the teacher to help the students solve the problem stated in the student question. For example, regarding the first question, "What do I want to learn?", the associated Teacher Objectives comprise the activities in which students should be engaged to answer the question. In this case, that involves helping students (a) identify their specific strengths and instructional needs; (b) identify and communicate preferences, interests, beliefs, and values; and (c) prioritize their instructional needs. As teachers use the model, they can likely generate more objectives that are relevant to the question, and they are encouraged to do so.

The student-directed instructional strategies and educational supports used in the model provide another means of teaching students to teach themselves. As important as this is, however, not every instructional strategy implemented will

(*text continues on p. 58*)

The Self-Determined Learning Model of Instruction:
Student Questions – Phase 1 – Set a Goal

Name ______________________________ Date ____________________
(Date Phase 1 Began)
School ______________________________

What is my goal? ➡ Let's try to identify something that you want to learn or improve on.

Please answer the questions below.

1. What do I want to learn or improve on?

____

____

____

↓

2. What do I know about it now?

____

____

____

↓

3. What must change for me to learn what I don't know?

____

____

____

↓

4. What can I do to make this happen?

____

____

____

➡ I have listed a specific, measurable activity for student question 4. This is my goal, the activity I will be working on during Phase 2 and Phase 3.

End of Phase 1

Go on to Phase 2 ➡

(continues)

Figure 8.2. The Self-Determined Learning Model of Instruction—Sample Student Worksheets (Wehmeyer et al., 2003; reprinted with permission).

The Self-Determined Learning Model of Instruction:
Student Questions – Phase 2 – Take Action

Name ______________________ Date ______________
(Date Phase 2 Began)
School ______________________

What is my plan? ➡ **Let's think about how to achieve the goal that you set.**

Please answer the questions below.

5. What can I do to learn what I don't know?

____
____
____

↓

6. What could keep me from taking action?

____
____
____

↓

7. What can I do to remove these barriers?

____
____
____

↓

8. When will I take action?

____
____
____

➡ End of Phase 2. I will start working on my plan and then go on to Phase 3.

End of Phase 2
Go on to Phase 3 ➡

(continues)

Figure 8.2. *(continued)*

The Self-Determined Learning Model of Instruction:
Student Questions – Phase 3 – Adjust Goal or Plan

Name ____________________ Date ____________________
(Date Phase 3 Began)
School ____________________

What have I learned? ➡ Let's think about whether or not you achieved your goal.

9. What actions have I taken?

____

____

⬇

10. What barriers have been removed?

____

____

⬇

11. What has changed about what I don't know?

____

____

⬇

12. Do I know what I want to know?

____

____

Did I finish my goal? Please mark in the bubble ◯ Yes ◯ No

If YES

How did I feel about the results?

____

____

➡ Now I will go back to Phase 1 and set a new goal.

If NO

➡ I will look back at Phase 1 again. If the goal is still a good one for me, I will move on to **Phase 2** to revise my plan **OR** I can rewrite my same goal or change it to a new goal.

Figure 8.2. *(continued)*

be student directed. The purpose of any model of teaching is to promote student learning and growth. However, there are circumstances in which the most effective instructional method to achieve a particular educational outcome involves using a teacher-directed strategy. Students who are considering what plan of action to implement to achieve a self-selected goal can recognize that teachers have expertise in instructional strategies and take full advantage of that expertise. The use of the SDLMI provides students with opportunities to learn to ask for help and to recognize how to balance directing their own learning with recruiting necessary supports and enabling others to direct learning when they have more expertise.

Creating Opportunities for Students to Use the Self-Determined Learning Model of Instruction

As mentioned previously, the SDLMI can be used to target many types of goals, and it can be beneficial for students to use the SDLMI across curricular areas. When the SDLMI has been used in academic content areas, it has been shown to improve academic-goal attainment as well as access to the general education curriculum. In this context, teachers can use the SDLMI one on one with students, or on a class-wide basis. Teachers often create "miniunits" on self-determination skills (e.g., what is a goal, what is a problem, teaching self-monitoring skills) so that students are both learning the skills necessary to set and achieve their own goals as well as receiving the traditional curriculum content they would have otherwise received. Often students need support to understand what an appropriate academic goal might be for them, particularly if they do not know their strengths and instructional needs in the academic area. However, research with the SDLMI has shown that, with instruction that enables students to identify what they know and do not know, students can set appropriate goals and make progress on these goals. Further, teachers begin to see students as more capable and having more opportunities to direct their learning, which takes some of the responsibility from teachers to always be setting goals.

Students can also use the SDLMI in other areas, like in learning transition skills or social skills. For example, for transition skills, a student might set a goal to improve his or her performance of a specific job skill during vocational experience (e.g., maybe he or she needs an antecedent cue regulation system to help complete the steps of an activity). Or, perhaps a student needs to learn how to solve problems that do not have an immediate solution on the job site (e.g., what to do if an item is in the wrong place on the shelf). The student might then work with his or her teacher to develop an action plan. Similarly, with social skills, students might—with support from their teacher—set goals related to building friendships or doing additional social activities with peers. It is important to remember that as a teacher or support person, you can provide input and feedback on student goals and action plans. The intent is not for the student to do this independently. However, the roles change from directing the goal to facilitating the student's identification of the goal and advocating for the student to have high expectations and access to the supports needed to set and go after his or her goals.

9 Conclusion

As described in the Introduction, *self-determination* is defined as acting as the causal agent in one's life, and this ability develops over the life span as children and youth have opportunities to engage in self-determined action: developing choice-making skills, decision-making and problem-solving skills, self-advocacy skills, goal-setting and -attainment skills, self-regulation and self-management skills, and self-awareness and self-knowledge.

The strategies discussed in this book can be used and modified to support students with ASD across their educational career, and they provide the foundations for success in adulthood and throughout life. There are multiple avenues through which to teach skills leading to enhanced self-determination, while attending to age/ability considerations and support needs. Multicomponent interventions, such as the Self-Determined Learning Model of Instruction, provide a means to teach and target multiple skills simultaneously, affecting both student skills and teacher instruction. Beginning instruction early to promote skills, knowledge, and beliefs leading to later self-determination and promoting it consistently across the student's educational career can significantly affect post-school outcomes for adolescents and young adults with ASD, as higher levels of self-determination have been linked with positive post-school outcomes, including increased employment and community integration.

There are multiple situations in which teachers and others can promote self-determination, and ideas for such were highlighted throughout this text. Almost any academic-, vocational-, or transition-related task provides natural opportunities for teaching goal-setting, problem-solving, choice-making, self-management, self-advocacy, and leadership skills. It is important to explore opportunities in extracurricular, community, and disability-related activities, as well. Carter, Sweeden, Walter, Moss, and Hsin (2011) interviewed young adults with disabilities about the development of leadership skills, and one of the clear and consistent findings was that young adults valued opportunities across to learn and practice skills leading to self-determination in all domains of life, and felt this access to multiple opportunities was what enabled them to become self-determined and develop leadership skills.

As a teacher or support person, a key aspect of supporting the development of self-determination is planning for repeated opportunities to learn and practice skills, such as those described in this text, and coordinating across home and school will enable students to have more opportunities to develop and expand their experiences and expectations for themselves. Expectations are a critical part of instruction to promote self-determination. Planning with high expectations is important to ensure that instruction is challenging and so that students develop action-control beliefs. People with disabilities have repeatedly identified the barriers that low expectations and restricted opportunities introduce. If children and youth with ASD do not have opportunities to explore the various options that are available to them, they cannot effectively express preferences and make choices, limiting their ability to engage in basic self-determined actions. At times, the attitudes of others about what people with ASD can and cannot do can be limiting. Research has found that promoting self-determination affects not only students' but also teachers' perceptions of students' capacity. For example, researchers have found that teachers, after implementing the Self-Determined Learning Model of Instruction, showed significant changes in their perceptions of students' capacity for self-determination (Shogren, Plotner, Palmer, Wehmeyer, & Paek, 2014). Essentially, teachers, after giving students opportunities to develop skills related to expressing their self-determination, came to see students as having greater capacity for self-determination, suggesting that teachers' attitudes and expectations changed as well. Thus, it is important for students with ASD and those that support them to see the possibilities of promoting self-determination and the capacities that students have for being self-determined when given opportunities to do so.

References

Agran, M., King-Sears, M., Wehmeyer, M. L., & Copeland, S. R. (2003). *Teachers' guides to inclusive practices: Student-directed learning strategies.* Baltimore, MD: Paul H. Brookes.

Agran, M., & Krupp, M. (2011). Providing choice making in employment programs: The beginning or end of self-determination? *Education and Training in Autism and Developmental Disabilities, 46,* 565–575.

Algozzine, B., Browder, D., Karvonen, M., Test, D. W., & Wood, W. M. (2001). Effects of interventions to promote self-determination for individuals with disabilities. *Review of Educational Research, 71,* 219–277. doi:10.3102/00346543071002219

Bauminger, N. (2007). Brief report: Individual social-multi-modal Intervention for HFASD. *Journal of Autism and Developmental Disorders, 37,* 1593–1604.

Benjamin, C. (1996). *Problem solving in school.* Upper Saddle River, NJ: Globe Fearon.

Beyth-Marom, R., Fischhoff, B., Quadrel, M. J., & Furby, L. (1991). Teaching decision making to adolescents: A critical review. In J. Baron & R. V. Brown (Eds.), *Teaching decision making to adolescents* (pp. 19–59). Hillsdale, NJ: Lawrence Erlbaum.

Carter, E. W., Swedeen, B., Walter, M. J., Moss, C. K., & Hsin, C.-T. (2011). Perspectives of young adults with disabilities on leadership. *Career Development for Exceptional Individuals, 34*(1), 57–67.

Chang, R., Durham, J., & Little, T. D. (in press). Enhancing students' motivation with autonomy-supportive classrooms. In M. L. Wehmeyer, K. A. Shogren, T. D. Little, & S. J. Lopez (Eds.), *Handbook on the development of self-determination.* New York, NY: Springer.

Chou, Y.-C., Wehmeyer, M. L., Palmer, S. B., & Lee, J. H. (in press). Comparisons of self-determination among students with autism, intellectual disability, and learning disabilities: A multivariate analysis. *Focus on Autism and Other Developmental Disabilities.*

Cobb, R. B., Lehmann, J., Newman-Gonchar, R., & Alwell, M. (2009). Self-determination for students with disabilities: A narrative metasynthesis. *Career Development for Exceptional Individuals, 32,* 108–114. doi:10.1177/0885728809336654

Dominguez, P. R., Gamiz, F., Gil, M., Moreno, H., Zamora, R. M., Gallo, M., & Brugada, I. (2013). Providing choice increases children's vegetable intake. *Food Quality and Preference, 30,* 108–113.

Faherty, C. (2000). *What does it mean to me? A workbook explaining self-awareness and life lessons to the child or youth with high functioning autism or Asperger's.* Arlington, TX: Future Horizons.

Hagopian, L. P., Long, E. S., & Rush, K. S. (2004). Preference assessment procedures for individuals with developmental disabilities. *Behavior Modification, 28,* 668–677. doi: 10.1177/0145445503259836

Held, M. F., Thoma, C. A., & Thomas, K. (2004). "The John Jones Show": How one teacher facilitate self-determined transition planning for a young man with autism. *Focus on Autism and Other Developmental Disabilities, 19,* 177–188.

Hickson, L., & Khemka, I. (2013). Problem solving and decision making. In M. L. Wehmeyer (Ed.), *The Oxford handbook of positive psychology and disability* (pp. 198–225). New York, NY: Oxford University Press.

Lee, S. H., Simpson, R. L., & Shogren, K. A. (2007). Effects and implications of self-management for students with autism: A meta-analysis. *Focus on Autism and Other Developmental Disabilities, 22*, 2–13.

Locke, E. A., & Latham, G. P. (2006). New directions in goal-setting theory. *Current Directions in Psychological Science, 15*, 265–268. doi:10.1111/j.1467-8721.2006.00449.x

Martin, J. E., Huber Marshall, L., & Sale, P. (2004). A 3-year study of middle, junior, high, and high school IEP meetings. *Exceptional Children, 70*, 285–297.

Martin, J. E., & Marshall, L. H. (1995). ChoiceMaker: A comprehensive self-determination transition program. *Intervention in School and Clinic, 30*, 147–156.

Reid, D. H., Parsons, M. B., & Green, C. W. (1991). *Providing choices and preferences for persons who have severe handicaps*. Morganton, NC: Habilitative Management.

Shevin, M., & Klein, N. K. (1984). The importance of choice-making skills for students with severe disabilities *Journal of the Association for Persons with Severe Handicaps, 9*, 159–166.

Shogren, K. A., Lang, R., Machalicek, W., Rispoli, M., & O'Reilly, M. F. (2011). Self versus teacher management of behavior for elementary school students with Asperger syndrome: Impact on classroom behavior. *Journal of Postive Behavior Interventions, 13*, 87–96. doi:10.1177/1098300710384508

Shogren, K. A., Lee, J. H., & Panko, P. (2016). Examining the relationship between autonomy, psychological empowerment, and self-realization and postschool outcomes. (Manuscript submitted for publication.)

Shogren, K. A., & Plotner, A. J. (2012). Characteristics of transition planning for students with disabilities: Data from the National Longitudinal Transition Study-2. *Intellectual and Developmental Disabilities, 50*, 16–30. doi:10.1352/1934-9556-50.1.16

Shogren, K. A., Plotner, A. J., Palmer, S. B., Wehmeyer, M. L., & Paek, Y. (2014). Impact of the Self-Determined Learning Model of Instruction on teacher perceptions of student capacity and opportunity for self-determination. *Education and Training in Autism and Developmental Disabilities, 49*, 440–448.

Shogren, K. A., Wehmeyer, M. L., Palmer, S. B., Forber-Pratt, A., Little, T. J., & Lopez, S. J. (2015). Causal agency theory: Reconceptualizing a functional model of self-determination. *Education and Training in Autism and Developmental Disabilities, 50*, 251–263.

Shogren, K. A., Wehmeyer, M. L., Little, T. J., Forber-Pratt, A., Palmer, S. B., & Seo, H. (2017). Preliminary validity and reliability of scores on the Self-Determination Inventory: Student Report version. *Career Development and Transition for Exceptional Individuals, (40)* 2. doi:10.1177/2165143415594335

Shogren, K. A., Wehmeyer, M. L., Palmer, S. B., Rifenbark, G. G., & Little, T. D. (2015). Relationships between self-determination and postschool outcomes for youth with disabilities. *Journal of Special Education, 53*, 30–41. doi:10.1177/0022466913489733

Test, D. W., Fowler, C. H., Wood, W. M., Brewer, D. M., & Eddy, S. (2005). A conceptual framework of self-advocacy for students with disabilities. *Remedial and Special Education, 26*, 43–54.

Test, D. W., Mazzotti, V. L., Mustian, A. L., Fowler, C. H., Kortering, L., & Kohler, P. (2009). Evidence-based secondary transition predictors for improving postschool outcomes for students with disabilities. *Career Development for Exceptional Individuals, 32*, 160–181. doi:10.1177/0885728809346960

Trainor, A. A. (2005). Self-determination perceptions and behaviors of diverse students with LD during the transition planning process. *Journal of Learning Disabilities, 38*, 233–248.

Wehmeyer, M. L., Agran, M., Hughes, C., Martin, J. E., Mithaug, D., & Palmer, S. (2007). *Promoting self-determination in students with developmental disabilities.* New York, NY: Guilford Press.
Wehmeyer, M. L., & Kelchner, K. (1995). *The Arc's self-determination scale.* Arlington, TX: The Arc National Headquarters.
Wehmeyer, M. L., Lawrence, M., Kelchner, K., Palmer, S. B., Garner, N., & Soukup, J. H. (2004). *Whose future is it anyway? A student-directed transition planning process.* Lawrence, KS: Kansas University Center on Developmental Disabilities.
Wehmeyer, M. L., Palmer, S. B., Agran, M., Mithaug, D. E., & Martin, J. E. (2000). Promoting causal agency: The Self-Determined Learning Model of Instruction. *Exceptional Children, 66,* 439–453.
Wehmeyer, M. L., Palmer, S. B., Shogren, K. A., Williams-Diehm, K., & Soukup, J. H. (2013). Establishing a causal relationship between interventions to promote self-determination and enhanced student self-determination. *Journal of Special Education, 46,* 195–210. doi:10.1177/0022466910392377
Wehmeyer, M. L., & Shogren, K. A. (in press-a). Applications of the self-determination construct to disability. In M. L. Wehmeyer, K. A. Shogren, T. D. Little, & S. J. Lopez (Eds.), *Handbook on the development of self-determination.* New York, NY: Springer.
Wehmeyer, M. L., & Shogren, K. A. (in press-b). Decision making. In M. L. Wehmeyer, K. A. Shogren, T. D. Little, & S. J. Lopez (Eds.), *Handbook on the development of self-determination.* New York, NY: Springer.
Wehmeyer, M. L., Shogren, K. A., Palmer, S., Garner, N., Lawrence, M., Soukup, J., . . . Kelly, J. (2003). *The Self-Determined Learning Model of Instruction: A teacher's guide.* Lawrence, KS: Beach Center on Disability, University of Kansas.
Wehmeyer, M. L., Shogren, K. A., Palmer, S. B., Williams-Diehm, K., Little, T. D., & Boulton, A. (2012). Impact of the Self-Determined Learning Model of Instruction on student self-determination: A randomized-trial placebo control group study. *Exceptional Children, 78,* 135–153.
Wehmeyer, M. L., Shogren, K. A., Zager, D., Smith, T. E. C., & Simpson, R. (2010). Research-based principles and practices for educating students with autism: Self-determination and social interactions. *Education and Training in Autism and Developmental Disabilities, 45,* 475–486.
Whitman, T. L. (1990). Self-regulation and mental retardation. *American Journal on Mental Retardation, 94*(4), 347–362.
Williams-Diehm, K., Wehmeyer, M. L., Palmer, S. B., Soukup, J., & Garner, N. (2008). Self-determination and student involvement in transition planning: A multivariate analysis. *Journal on Developmental Disabilities, 14,* 27–39.
Wolman, J., Campeau, P., Dubois, P., Mithaug, D., & Stolarski, V. (1994). *AIR Self-Determination Scale and user guide.* Palo Alto, CA: American Institute for Research.
Zimmerman, B. J., & Kitsantas, A. (1999). Acquiring writing revision skill: Shifting from process to outcome self-regulatory goals. *Journal of Educational Psychology, 91*(2), 241–250. doi:10.1037/0022-0663.91.2.241

Appendix

Additional Online Resources

National Gateway to Self-Determination
www.ngsd.org

National Technical Assistance Center on Transition
www.transitionta.org

Self-Determination Inventory System
www.self-determination.org

Zarrow Center for Learning Enrichment—Self-Determination Assessment Tools
www.ou.edu/content/education/centers-and-partnerships/zarrow/self-determination-assessment-tools.html

Zarrow Center for Learning Enrichment—ChoiceMaker Self-Determination Curriculum
www.ou.edu/content/education/centers-and-partnerships/zarrow/choicemaker-curriculum.html

About the Editor and Authors

Richard L. Simpson was professor emeritus, University of Kansas. During his more than 40 years as a professor of special education at the University of Kansas, he directed numerous demonstration programs for students with autism spectrum disorder (ASD) and other disabilities and coordinated a variety of federal grant programs related to students with ASD and other disabilities. He also worked as a teacher of students with disabilities, a psychologist, and an administrator of programs for students with autism. He was the former editor of the professional journal *Focus on Autism and Other Developmental Disabilities* (published by the Hammill Institute on Disabilities) and the author of numerous books and articles on ASD.

Karrie A. Shogren, PhD, is a Professor in the Department of Special Education, Senior Scientist in the Life Span Institute, and Director of the Kansas University Center on Developmental Disabilities, all at the University of Kansas. Dr. Shogren's research focuses on self-determination and systems of support for students with disabilities. Dr. Shogren has published over 125 articles in peer-reviewed journals, is the author or coauthor of 10 books, and is one of the coauthors of *Intellectual Disability: Definition, Classification, and Systems of Support,* the eleventh edition of the American Association on Intellectual and Developmental Disabilities' seminal definition of intellectual disability, as well as the *Supports Intensity Scale–Children's and Adult Version.* Dr. Shogren has received grant funding from several sources, including the Institute of Education Sciences (IES) and the National Institute on Disability, Independent Living, and Rehabilitation Research (NIDILRR). Dr. Shogren is coeditor of the journal *Inclusion and Remedial and Special Education.*

Michael L. Wehmeyer, PhD, is the Ross and Marianna Beach Distinguished Professor in Special Education and Chairperson, Department of Special Education; and Director and Senior Scientist, Beach Center on Disability within the Schiefelbusch Institute for Life Span Studies, all at the University of Kansas. Dr. Wehmeyer is the author or coauthor of more than 375 peer-reviewed journal articles or book chapters and has authored, coauthored, edited, or coedited

36 books on disability and education-related issues, including issues pertaining to self-determination, positive psychology and disability, transition to adulthood, the education and inclusion of students with severe disabilities, and technology use by people with cognitive disabilities. He is coauthor of the widely used textbook *Exceptional Lives: Special Education in Today's Schools*, published by Merrill/ Prentice Hall, now in its eighth edition. Dr. Wehmeyer is a past president of the Board of Directors for and a Fellow of the American Association on Intellectual and Developmental Disabilities (AAIDD); a past president of the Council for Exceptional Children's (CEC) Division on Career Development and Transition (DCDT); a Fellow of the American Psychological Association (APA), Intellectual and Developmental Disabilities Division (Div. 33); Vice President of the CEC Division on Autism and Developmental Disabilities (DADD); and past vice president for the American Association and a Fellow of the International Association for the Scientific Study of Intellectual and Developmental Disabilities (IASSIDD). He is former editor-in-chief of the journal *Remedial and Special Education* and is a founding coeditor of the AAIDD journal *Inclusion*. He is a coauthor of the *AAIDD Supports Intensity Scale* and the 2010 *AAIDD Intellectual Disability Terminology, Classification, and Systems of Supports Manual.*